# CHEESE

### BY
## AUDREY M DUDSON

### ILLUSTRATIONS BY
## HELEN S COOPER

Published by Dudson Publications Limited,
200 Scotia Road, Tunstall, Stoke-on-Trent, Staffordshire ST6 4JD.

Distributed by Richard Dennis Publications,
The Old Chapel, Middle Street, Shepton Beauchamp,
Nr Ilminster, Somerset TA19 0LE.

Printed and Produced in Great Britain by Osborne Publicity Services Limited,
Corbar Hall, Corbar Road, Buxton, Derbyshire SK17 6TF .

ISBN 0-9510126-1-4

# ACKNOWLEDGEMENTS

I am extremely indebted to the following for allowing me access to their archives:
The Trustees of the Wedgwood Museum, Barlaston, Stoke-on-Trent, Staffordshire, England.
The Spode Museum Trust, Stoke-on-Trent.
Royal Doulton (UK) Ltd, Burslem, Stoke-on-Trent.
Moorcroft plc, Burslem, Stoke-on-Trent, Miss Beatrice and Mr Walter Moorcroft.
Burgess & Leigh Ltd, Burslem, Stoke-on-Trent, Mr Barry Leigh.
The Denby Pottery Company Ltd, Denby, Derbyshire, Mr Stephen Riley.
Blakeney Art Pottery, Stoke-on-Trent, Mr Michael Bailey.

My very sincere thanks to members of the following Museums for valuable help so willingly given:
The Birmingham Museums & Art Gallery, Chamberlain Square, Birmingham.
Mrs P Halfpenny & Mrs K Niblett at the City Museum & Art Gallery, Hanley, Stoke-on-Trent.
Mrs V Baynton & Mrs K Ellis at the Royal Doulton Museum, Burslem, Stoke-on-Trent.
The Gladstone Pottery Museum, Longton, Stoke-on-Trent.
Mrs C F Walker, Hornsea Museum, 11 Newbegin, Hornsea, N Humberside.
Mrs J Jones and the staff at the Minton Museum, Royal Doulton Ltd, Stoke-on-Trent.
Mr R J Wyatt, Division of Museum Services, Sands Point Preserve, 95 Middleneck Road, Port Washington, N Y 11050, USA.
Mr R Copeland at the Spode Museum, Spode Ltd, Stoke-on-Trent.
Miss G Blake Roberts and Mrs L Miller at the Wedgwood Museum, Barlaston, Stoke-on-Trent.
Also the Stilton Cheese Makers' Association, Buxton, Derbyshire and the Good Housekeeping Institute, London.

I greatly appreciate the assistance I have had from the following: Ms V Bergesen, Mr H Blakeney, Mr N Dawes, Mr K Edwards, Dr D Furniss, Mr & Mrs R Hampson, Ms A Kelly, Mr G Leggatt, Mrs O Middleton, Mr J Gordon Miller of Harrods Ltd, Mr H Sandon, The Earl Spencer, Mr A Townsend, Dr G M Urquhart.

Photographs have kindly been provided by collectors in many parts of the world. Their contributions have provided valuable information and are much appreciated. Detailed information was not always provided and so sizes and marks were not always available; they have been stated where possible.

I am especially grateful to Dr Marilyn Karmason for supplying and allowing me to reproduce photographs from her Majolica book; to Mrs Matthews of Derbyshire for allowing us to photograph her collection; to my daughter-in-law Carol Dudson for word-processing my untidy longhand and to my sister-in-law Helen Cooper for her talented illustrations.

Acknowledgements, however, would not be complete without very special thanks to two collectors who have made outstanding contributions to the photography. I am not only grateful to them for photographing their collections but also for their special co-operation – Mrs Adele Entwistle and Mr Brian Atkinson.

# CONTENTS

# FOREWORD

Food and drink are fundamental to human existence, but over the years their consumption has become much more than the maintenance of life. It has become an art form, never more so than in the ceramic items produced to enhance the presentation of a special delicacy. Nearly everybody can remember the cheese dish which adorned their parents' or grandparents' sideboard, a functional yet often a highly decorative addition to the dining room. These unique forms have always provided a fascinating aspect of ceramic factory production and this well researched book expresses not only the varying shapes but their relationship to the changing social habits of the past.

Any collector will be enchanted by the careful research and detailed information provided on each individual manufactory's production of cheese dishes, a subject which has never been tackled in detail before. The large number of illustrations from world-wide sources add immensely to this new work which will be a must for all ceramic collections and a useful and valuable addition to every library.

February 1993

**Gaye Blake Roberts** FMA, FRSA
Curator, Wedgwood Museum

i

# PREFACE

It is virtually impossible to find detailed information on cheese dishes - or cheese stands as they were generally called by the pottery industry - from a single source of reference. Books about antiques, even those dealing specifically with ceramics, contain only occasional reference and rarely are they included in the Illustrated Price Guides. Yet cheese stands have become much collected in the last twenty years. Two articles have been written recently giving very interesting, general background history but are not specific enough for the dedicated collector.[1]

The reason for this dearth of information becomes obvious when the subject is studied more deeply - it is not easy to obtain. However, thanks to the co-operation of the various pottery manufacturers, who have generously allowed access to their archives, new information has been collected from their early shape books, pattern books and old catalogues. Unfortunately, in the case of many factories, records are no longer in existence and advertisements in the 19th century and early 20th century trade journals are not often accompanied by photographs therefore many of the cheese stands cannot be identified and have to remain "manufacturer unknown." But the dishes are very pretty and which factory made them is not the only important factor, interesting as it is.

The more fascinating story, which this investigation makes possible, is the development of cheese stands through nearly two centuries together with the factors which influenced their popularity and their various forms of decoration, shape and design.

*(1) Marshall Cavendish's TIMES PAST 1988 (P406-8)*
*A La Carte Magazine November 1986*

# INTRODUCTION

Cheese has played an important part in the British diet for many years and by the early 18th century many types of regional cheeses were being made. Their characteristics differed due to the breed of cattle supplying the milk, variations in the type of pasture on which they grazed and the fact that cheese making was essentially a rural and variable function. For example the extent and duration of renneting, the cutting of the curd and the subsequent pressure applied. However, towards the end of the 1760s it became a fashionable pastime of the rich to pretend they were dairymaids. To have a tiled dairy fully equipped with matching utensils such as milk settling pans, cream vases and cream strainers became a status symbol, especially if the equipment was adorned with the family crest. The cream strainer shown in Plate 1 is decorated in brown enamel on glaze with the crest of the Palk family of Haldon House in Devonshire.

Josiah Wedgwood's creamware was considered ideal for dairy ware and his special equipment included not only strainers, skimmers, dairy spoons, butter kits, whey cups, covers and stands (Fig 1) but also tiles to match.

It is often thought that Marie Antoinette, with her make-believe village, le Hameau at Versailles, set the fashion but in fact the taste for elegant but practical dairies was well established in England some years earlier than this.[2] In 1789 Lavinia, Lady Spencer, gave her order to Wedgwood for her dairy at Althorp in Northamptonshire and this dairy is still complete. This is the ancestral home of Lady Diana Spencer, now Princess of Wales.

2) *"Decorative Wedgwood in Architecture and Furniture" by Alison Kelly.*
*Born-Hawkes Publishing Ltd, New York 1965*

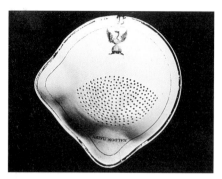

Plate 1 Cream Strainer decorated on glaze in brown enamel. Impressed WEDGWOOD c.1776 - 1800. 19.7 cm wide. (Courtesy the Buten Collection of the Decorative Arts Library - Nassau County Division of Museum Services. Sands Point Preserve, Port Washington, N Y, USA)

Plate 2 Endsleigh Dairy Cream Vase. Hand painted creamware for the Duke of Bedford's dairy. The lids have a central hole for cooling. Impressed WEDGWOOD c.1795. 40 cm high.(Courtesy Buten Collection USA)

Fig 1 A page from the Charles Gill Travellers' Notebook showing Wedgwood Dairy equipment (p 69) watermarked 1811. (Courtesy the Trustees of the Wedgwood Museum, Barlaston, Stoke-on-Trent, England)

Fig 2 Lady Spencer's dairy 1786 reproduced from Alison Kelly's book (see footnote 2). (Courtesy The Earl Spencer)

The tiles and cream vases are decorated with dark green ivy trails and the milk pans have a narrow green line. (Fig 2) (Plate 2 Cream Vase)

Figure 3 shows a Wedgwood cheese mould. This was lined with cheese cloth and the perforations allowed excessive moisture to escape and the curds and cream to solidify into a block of cheese.

Reference has already been made to the fact that variation in local conditions resulted in regional cheeses having their own characteristics, some soft cheeses, others hard, such as Cheddar, Cheshire and double Gloucester. One cheese, however, comes into a category of its own, namely the blue veined Stilton cheese, sometimes called the King of English cheese.

In his "Tour through England and Wales" in 1727 Daniel Defoe stated that he passed through Stilton, a town famous for cheese. From the 1720s Stilton cheese had been supplied to the Bell Inn, a coaching inn on the Great North Road, at Stilton in Huntingdonshire, and travellers spread word of the excellent cheese which had been served to them. This inn is still in existence today and has recently been extensively renovated. (Plate 3)

There is an element of doubt as to the origin of this cheese but credit is generally given to Mrs Elizabeth Orton who was house-keeper at Quenby Hall in Leicestershire. She taught her daughter, Mrs Paulet, a farmer's wife, to make the cheese also. Mrs Orton's other daughter married Cowper Thornhill, who was the landlord of the Bell Inn, and he received supplies of the cheese from his sister-in-law. The cheese was originally called "Quenby" but the early coach travellers gave it the name "Stilton". Stilton cheese has been made in Leicestershire and also at Hartington in Derbyshire for generations, first by farming families and later by small dairy companies. Today production is limited to the three counties of Leicestershire, Derbyshire and Nottinghamshire as the Stilton certification trademark is vested in the Stilton Cheese Makers' Association. (Fig 4) This association came into being in 1936 and helped to evolve modern dairy methods.

White Stilton is sold young before the veining has had time to develop but for blue Stilton the cheeses are placed in a ripening room for three months to allow the blue veins to appear. This process is natural and is promoted by allowing the oxygen in the atmosphere to enter the cheese through holes made in it with stainless steel needles. This allows a mould of the penicillin type to grow naturally in the cheese.[3]

By the end of the 18th century the demand for Stilton had grown, as it had for all the other great regional cheeses. Messrs Paxton and Whitfield opened a cheese shop in Jermyn Street, London, followed by cheese shops elsewhere in the country. Lightweight, but very strong baskets, with a carrying handle and a toggle for fastening, were handmade in English willow to transport the cheeses to these new cheese shops and to local markets. (Plate 4)

*Plate 3.* The Bell Inn at Stilton near Peterborough as it is today. (Courtesy Osborne Publicity Services Ltd)

(3) *Osborne Publicity Services Ltd on behalf of the Stilton Cheese Makers' Association, Buxton, Derbyshire.*

# EARLY SERVICE OF CHEESE

In the late 17th century and during the 18th century whole cheeses were usually served on plain, wooden platters known as trenchers. Sometimes, for heavy cheeses, these were made to revolve and sometimes they were made as wooden coasters i.e. shallow wooden dishes with wheels of either brass or leather which could be pushed along the table. Towards the end of the 18th century special dishes were made for serving cheese. These were also of wood, especially mahogany, and were in the shape of a cradle. Plate 6 shows one that rotates on its base while Plate 5 shows one which completely encloses the cheese to restrain its smell. Often these wooden cradles had an off-centre internal division so that two different round, flat cheeses of varying thicknesses could be served or alternatively bread could be placed in one side. These, too, were sometimes mounted on wheels.

By the end of the 18th century the demand for cheese had greatly increased and several pottery manufacturers, noting this new gastronomic trend, felt that something more elegant should be produced to replace the old wooden cradles. A few silver cradles had been produced by Edward Wakelin in 1760 and John Parker in 1764 but these were very expensive. Wedgwood and Spode led the way in catering for this new market and offered a variety of shapes in earthenware.

## Flat or Footed Cheesestands

Around the turn of the century, dishes of this shape were produced by several manufacturers sometimes being referred to as cheesestands or cake stands. Obviously they could be used for both purposes but the early extant archives lead one to the conclusion that they were primarily intended for cheese. Among the early manufacturers Wedgwood and Spode predominated. Four of Josiah Wedgwood's early shapes (c.1800) are shown in Figure 5, while Figure 6 illustrates the Spode variation. Josiah Spode perfected the technique of underglaze transfer printing, mainly on pearlware, about this time and the well-known Spode blue prints can be found on their dishes. The cheese stand shown in Plate 7 is decorated with the rare "Flower Cross" pattern. It is unmarked but this appears to be a design used solely by Spode; usually the Spode dishes are impressed SPODE.

Dishes of this type were admired for their elegance and remained popular until the mid 19th century. (Plate 8)

Copeland and Garrett took over the Spode works in 1833 and produced the cheese stand shown in Plate 9 which is from their Botanical Series. These dishes are sometimes referred to as Stilton Cheese Stands and obviously it was possible to use them in this way. It would, however, seem likely that they were more appropriate for the smaller regional cheeses, especially as covered dishes and stands were already being produced specifically for Stilton.

## Pottery Cradles

In addition to these round and oval cheese stands, pottery cradles were also produced to replace the old wooden ones. They were similar in shape but had a standing foot as can be seen in the illustration of the Don Factory shape. (Fig 11)

Around 1810 Spode produced a pottery cradle which, like Wedgwood's, took round, flat farmhouse cheeses. The centre decoration is from aquatint engravings of the castle and bridge of St. Angelo and Trajan's Column in Rome which appeared in *"Merigot's Views of Rome and its Vicinity"* published 1796 - 98.[4] (Plate 10)

The James and Ralph Clews' cheese cradle is very rare and is decorated with the print of "Dr Syntax and the Gypsies" (Plate 11) c.1820.

The two other examples, to which a manufacturer cannot be

(4) *Information supplied by Robert Copeland*

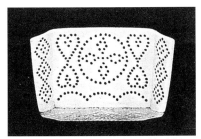

*Fig 3* Creamware octagonal mould which was lined with cheese cloth. Excess moisture escaped through the perforations leaving a solid block of cheese. Height 10 cm. Length 18.7 cm. Width 10 cm. (Courtesy Buten Collection USA)

*Fig 4* A map showing permitted Stilton cheese making areas. (Courtesy Stilton Cheese Makers' Association)

*Plate 4.* Traditional Stilton market baskets for either whole or half cheeses. (Courtesy Osborne Publicity Services Ltd)

*Plate 5* An 18th century, mahogany, enclosed cheese cradle. (Courtesy Birmingham City Council Museums & Art Gallery)

*Plate* 6 Wooden cheese cradle mahogany 18th century. (Courtesy Ford Green Hall Museum, Stoke-on-Trent)

*Plate* 7 Spode pearlware cheese stand decorated with the rare "Flower Cross" pattern unmarked c.1810-15.
 Diameter 27.8 cm. Height 4.4 cm. (Courtesy J Leatherland)

*Plate* 8 Wedgwood pearlware cheese stand decorated with the "Waterfall" pattern. Impressed WEDGWOOD c.1830. Diameter 30.3 cm. Height 7.5 cm. (Courtesy J Leatherland)

*Plate* 9 Copeland and Garrett cheese stand with decoration from their botanical series. Impressed COPELAND & GARRETT and also a printed mark c.1840. Diameter 28.4 cm. Height 4.4 cm. (Courtesy J Leatherland)

Plate 10 Spode pearlware cheese cradle, underglaze blue print "Rome." Impressed SPODE 1810-25  30 cm x 19.4 cm. (Courtesy Spode Museum Trust)

Plate 11 James & Ralph Clews' cheese cradle with underglaze blue print "Dr Syntax and the Gypsies." Impressed CLEWS 1820s. (Courtesy Griffin Antiques, Petworth)

Plate 12 Pottery cheese cradle, unmarked 1820-40. Height 17.8 cm. Length 42.2 cm. (Courtesy City Museum & Art Gallery, Stoke on Trent)

Plate 13 Pearlware "Willow" cheese cradle Unmarked 1820-40. Height 19.4 cm. Length 42.5 cm. Width 15.6 cm. (Courtesy City Museum & Art Gallery, Stoke on Trent)

Plate 14 Spode cream ware cheese stand with glass cover decorated with the W T Copeland coat-of-arms. Impressed SPODE c.1825. Cover height 20.5 cm. Diameter of plate 22.3 cm. (Courtesy Spode Museum Trust)

Plate 15 Spode Stilton cheese pan – underglaze blue "Italian" pattern on pearlware. Impressed SPODE c.1820. Diameter 26.2 cm. Height 10.5 cm. (Courtesy Spode Museum Trust) attributed, date between 1820-40. The cradle in Plate 12 is very porous, with discolouration due to staining by the cheese. It has a very pale blue underglaze transfer depicting a cottage with trees on a hillside while the print on the other cradle is much deeper blue. (Plate 13)

### Cheese boxes and tubs

Wedgwood produced cheese tubs; the earliest appears to have been made in 1794 in a plain cane coloured body, pierced at the base. This same tub, and also another hooped, unpierced and handled tub were still in production in a white earthenware body into the 1950s. (Fig 8)

### Cheese Toasters

Figure 7 shows three Wedgwood cheese toasters (shapes 1098, 1099 & 1100). The cheese toaster consisted of a shallow dish which was placed in a container of hot water over a hot plate. Mustard and seasonings were mixed into the cheese which was then stirred until melted. The dish was then put into a hot oven to brown the surface of the cheese.[5] Some cheese toasters had their own hot water reservoir i.e. they were made with three sections: base, inner plate and cover. The cheese mixture was sent to table over boiling water in the base because to quote Mrs Beeton in 1861[6] *"whichever way it [the cheese mixture] is served it is highly necessary that the mixture is very hot and very quickly sent to table or it will be worthless".*

An earlier method of using a cheese toaster is given in the following recipe of 1791.[7]

*Welch Rabbit*

*Cut a flice of bread a little wider than the cheefe, cut off the cruft, and toaft it on both fides; cut a flice of cheese moderately thick, put it in the cheefe toafter and toaft it on one fide, then put the toafted fide downwards on the bread and toaft the other fide; put pepper, falt and muftard over it, cut into pieces about an inch long and fend up quick.*

(5) *The Good Housekeeping Institute*
(6) *The Book of Household Management by Mrs Isabella Beeton 1861 and Maggie Black's assistance regarding copyright is gratefully acknowledged*
(7) *The English Art of Cookery by Richard Briggs 1791*

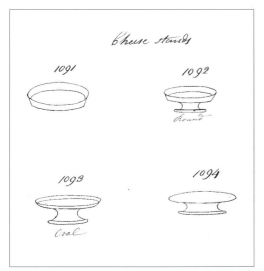

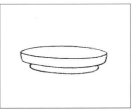

*Fig 5* Wedgwood flat or footed cheese stands c 1800. Part of a page from Shape book No 1 – watermarked 1802. (Wedgwood Museum Trust)

*Fig 6* Line drawing to show the shape of the Spode footed cheese stand c 1800. Diameter 27 cm. Height 5 cm.

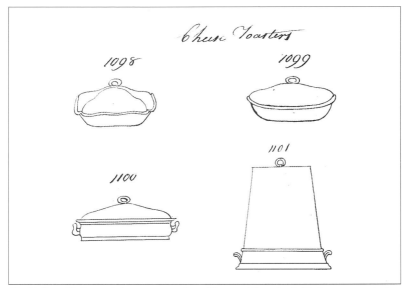

*Fig 7* .Three Wedgwood cheese toasters from Museum Shape book No 1 – watermarked 1802 (Wedgwood Museum Trust). Shape 1101 is one of Wedgwood's earliest Stilton cheese stands.

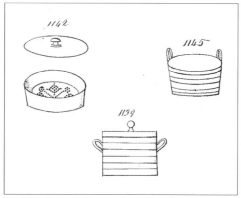

*Fig 8* Wedgwood cheese tubs – pierced and hooped made in cane, sage and white body – from Shape book No 1, watermarked 1802.
(Wedgwood Museum Trust)

*Fig 9* Wedgwood bas-relief Stilton cheese stand made in two sizes, large and small, in blue, sage and buff bodies with white sprigging. Shape book No 1, watermarked 1802. (Wedgwood Museum Trust)

*Fig 10* Minton footed cheese stand (NO 546) introduced c 1850 – featured in their 1884 Illustrated Catalogue of shapes M/S1336. (Courtesy Minton Archives, Royal Doulton Ltd)

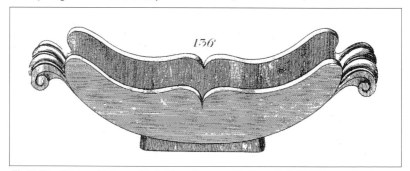

*Fig 11* Don Pottery, Swinton, Yorkshire, cheese cradle from their 1807 Pattern book.

# STILTON CHEESE STANDS
# UP TO 1850

S pecial containers for serving Stilton cheese were made from the beginning of the 19th century. Wedgwood was the first to produce a tall cylindrical cover with matching base plate as early as 1800 and offered three of these specialist dishes. (Figs 7,9,12) It was obviously desirable that Stilton should be kept covered not only to restrict drying but also to prevent the strong smell of the ripe cheese permeating the room. Because of the method of manufacture - Stilton is not pressed but is bound in cloth - the base plates of these dishes were made large enough to take the whole circumference of the cheese with the dome or cover tall enough to accommodate either the whole or fractions of the whole cheese. Josiah Wedgwood used the term *"cheese bell covers for stands,"* obviously this was inspired by their somewhat bell-like shape but it has also been suggested that the original association with the Bell Inn at Stilton played a part too.

Josiah Spode was unusual in offering glass domed cheese stands from c.1810. Spode manufactured the bases for these in creamware decorated with a wide variety of patterns, frequently botanical subjects, but the glass domes were not produced at the Spode factory. They were probably purchased in London as Spode was a dealer in glass. (Plate 14) He also produced deep covered containers called cheese pans which were specially made to retain the freshness of Stilton cheese. The bases of these were deeper than usual, 4 cm as opposed to the more normal 2.3 cm, so that the cheese was placed into the container rather than on it. (Plate 15 page 91)

In the 1840s Wedgwood was still supplying plain, round covers, sold separately in a variety of styles, primarily intended for a range of flat or footed stands as illustrated in Figure 5.

During the 1840s the railway network was established making the transportation of Stilton Cheese a great deal easier with a consequent upsurge in its popularity, so from the late 1840s onwards several manufacturers began competing in the market for cylindrical Stilton cheese stands. Copeland and Garrett, in the 1840s, produced a ribbed cheese stand in "Agate", a marbled decorative effect resembling the natural stone. (Fig 13) In 1850 Minton produced a plain cheese stand with a footed base plate - No 546 (Fig 13) and Wedgwood added a new plain shape "Ansty" to the range. "Ansty" was sold in three decorative forms: glazed white with gold, cane body, and in the newly introduced grey-blue coloured body called Lavender (Fig 14) - a few years later it was also Majolica glazed.

Fig 12 Wedgwood Stilton cheese stand from shape book No 1, watermarked 1802. (Wedgwood Museum Trust)

Fig 13 Copeland & Garrett ribbed cheese stand - "Agate" c.1840. This shape is also reproduced in their 1880s catalogue when it was produced in Stoneware and Parian. The "Agate" dish is marked with white pad mark R C 111. (From a catalogue at the Spode Museum)

Stilton Cheese Stand and Cover.

Fig 14 Wedgwood "Ansty" shape c.1850. This shape was still featured in their 1912 catalogue for Lavender Ware. (Wedgwood Museum Trust)

14

# STILTON CHEESE STANDS - 1850 ONWARDS

S o began the peak period for production of these stands and it was the Dudson factory which dominated this market throughout the second half of the 19th century, not so much in the quantity they produced but in the extensive range of patterns and colours. Jasper of course predominated, but the range of embossed stoneware and other decorative forms was also considerable and the quality high.

Not every manufacturer was tempted to produce this shape because great skill was needed both to make and fire them. They took up a considerable amount of space in the kiln during firing and it was extremely difficult to control the bottle ovens at a steady temperature - a very great deal depended upon the skill of the fireman. Losses must have been relatively high; consequently these dishes were expensive to make and obviously, therefore, to purchase. However, in spite of all these difficulties, the quality of cheese stands which were produced from 1850 to the 1890s was very high.

Many different forms of decoration are to be found on the stands and it is interesting to note how frequently the decoration was influenced by the Victorian fashions and tastes of each decade. It must be remembered, however, that once a shape or design had been modelled, if it proved popular, it was retained for several years, sometimes twenty or even more. By the 1850s popular interior decor consisted of heavy curtains, richly patterned wallpaper and solid furniture; if Stilton cheese stands were to satisfy current taste, and look at home standing on the large sideboards, they too had to be heavy and ornate. The Victorians loved their gardens and The Royal Horticultural

*Fig 15* Minton shape No 540 "Pompeiian" from Minton Museum shape book c.1850. (Courtesy Minton Museum, Royal Doulton Ltd)

*Fig 16* Minton shape No 809 "Ivy Embossed" from Minton Museum shape book c.1850.

*Fig 17* Minton shape No 862 "Hooped" from Minton Museum shape book c.1860.

Society of London had been formed in 1804 to encourage and improve Horticulture, both useful and ornamental. The Society held exhibitions and lectures and also organised plant hunting expeditions abroad. As a result many new species were introduced into Britain. This interest was reflected domestically. Well-loved flowers and plants, especially the many varieties of ferns which were so popular in the gardens and conservatories, were adapted as decoration on pottery, sometimes naturally, sometimes in a stylised manner. Birds and animals were also regarded as endearing and were frequently used for ornamentation.

In the 1870s and 1880s the Aesthetic Movement was the new influence which lead to a shift in public taste away from the solid, heavy and richly ornamented towards lighter, "more artistic" and elegant design. Bullrushes, peacock feathers, lilies and sunflowers were all symbols of this movement.

Also in the 1870/80s there was a great fashion for all things Japanese. Japan was only opened up to the West in the 1850s and Japanese art came as something of a revelation with its delicacy and pure, bright colours. The peacock came to epitomise all that was gorgeous while the crane appeared as a symbol of beauty. Perhaps the crane even outdistanced the sunflower as the hallmark of Aestheticism. The Japanese cult gave rise to a fashion for all kinds of Oriental art. When Liberty's, the famous London store in Regent Street, opened in 1875 it sold mainly Oriental goods - fabrics, bamboo furniture, screens and fans etc and this firm played a role in influencing new ideas in design.

The types of decorative treatment on these Stilton cheese stands falls roughly into six categories:-

1. Embossed or Relief moulded
2. Sprigged
3. Inlaid
4. Printed
5. Jet Ware & Terracotta
6. Majolica

**Embossed**

From early Victorian days relief decorated stoneware jugs were very popular, i.e. the decoration was part of the mould from

*Plate 16* Dudson White Stoneware "Hops, Vines & Wheat." Unmarked c.1850-90. Diameter 30.45 cm. Height 21.25 cm.

*Plate 17* Dudson White glazed Stoneware "Vertical Ferns." Unmarked c.1860-90. Diameter 26.8 cm. Height 22.5 cm.

*Plate 19* Unidentified White glazed Stoneware "Bamboo." Unmarked 1870s.

*Plate 18* Unidentified White Stoneware "Fig." Unmarked 1860-80.

which they were cast. From c.1850 this technique was applied to Stilton cheese stands also. The characteristics of embossed ware in the 1850s were well-defined floral decoration in high relief, sometimes in panels, or loose running plant patterns. Minton introduced "Pompeiian" c.1850 and "Ivy-Embossed" a few years later, and Dudson introduced their "Hops, Vines & Wheat" also in 1850. (Figs 15 & 16 and Plate 16)

Towards the end of the 1850s the fashion for heavily embossed cheese stands was beginning to fade and taste was turning towards lower-relief decoration and geometrical designs, such as Minton "Hooped" (Fig 17) and "Wicker" (Fig 18) both of which were introduced c.1860 also "Spiral" (shape No 3015) which they produced in the late 1870s. (Fig 19)

Production of both styles, to some extent, continued throughout the rest of the century but more especially those with lower relief, and manufacturers offered their models in "White glaze with or without gilding", in "White, coloured and gilt" (i.e. parts of the relief moulding were coloured), and some Majolica glazed stands. Factories such as Wedgwood, George Jones and Brownfield employed all three techniques. Dudson, as far as is known, did not produce Majolica cheese stands, instead the factory glazed the stands, which were made of white stoneware, with hand enamelled raised decoration. (Plates 17, 26, Colour Plates 1, 2) This form of decoration became popular with many firms in the late 1870s and throughout the '80s and presumably was offered as an alternative to Majolica "Argenta." French potters were producing relief moulded cheese dishes with cream grounds and the relief decorated with multi-coloured Majolica glazes. Many of these dishes were exported to England and the United States. Wedgwood's answer to this foreign competition was to produce "Argenta" Majolica cheese stands decorated in a similar manner but with a white back-ground. (see Plate 41 page 47)

Royal Worcester introduced relief moulded Stilton cheese stands in unglazed white Parian in c.1850s which are listed in their order books of that period but there are no illustrations and pieces were not marked.

*Fig 18* Minton shape No 763 "Wicker" embossed from Minton Museum shape book c.1860.

*Fig 19* Minton shape No 3015 "Spiral" footed cheese stand from Minton Museum shape book c.1879-1920s.

In the late 1870s Wedgwood changed the form of one of their cheese stands. Shape 1101 (as illustrated in Fig 7) was discontinued. Using the same shape number 1101, again a new shape was introduced which was included in the *"Illustrated Catalogue of Shapes 1880."* (Fig 20)

Demand for embossed cheese stands of cylindrical shape began to decline during the 1890s until it virtually ceased in 1900.

*Fig 20* Page from the Wedgwood 1880 "Illustrated Catalogue of Shapes" showing new shape 1101 introduced in the late 1870s.

*Fig 21* Copeland "Rutland" cheese stand from 1880s catalogue at the Spode Museum c.1860-90. Height 32.5 cm. (Courtesy Spode Museum Trust)

*Fig 22* Copeland "Caltha" cheese stand from 1880s catalogue at the Spode Museum c.1860-90.

*Fig 23* Copeland "Chelsea" cheese stand from the 1880s catalogue at the Spode Museum.

21

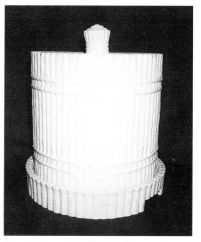

*Plate 20* Brownfield White glazed Stoneware "Tower." Impressed W B date impressed 8/77 1870-90. (Courtesy Harrods Ltd)

*Plate 21* Brownfield White Stoneware "Bamboo." Impressed W B 1870-90.

*Plate 23* Unattributed White Stoneware "Corn." Unmarked - not Copeland nor Dudson - possibly might be Bell & Co Ltd of Glasgow 1860/70.

*Plate 22* George Jones White glazed Stoneware "Apple Blossom." Unmarked 1870s. Half-size.

*Plate 24* Attributed to Ridgway - Blue Stoneware - also recorded in White and Sage. Unmarked. Height 27.5 cm. (Courtesy Phoenix Antiques)

*Plate 25* Minton - Blue line decoration over White glaze. Unmarked but identified as Shape No 862 1860.

*Plate 26* Dudson - enamelled on relief "Carnation" painted both inside cover and on base 9/67N/2 date impressed 10/79. Diameter 22 cm. Height 21.25 cm.

Fig 24 Minton Majolica shape No 620 "Mouse" late 1850s-80s. Height 12.5 cm. (Courtesy Minton Museum, Royal Doulton Ltd)

**Sprigged or Jasper Ware**

As is well known, Josiah Wedgwood was the originator of this decorative technique, which was developed after several years of experimentation in the 1770s. It was to become one of his most successful lines and he established a flourishing market for this type of ware. As always happens, even today, when a lucrative market is created other manufacturers produce their own versions with which to compete. Several firms did so but among the most notable were Adams, Copeland, Dudson, Ridgway and Turner. (Colour Plates 5 & 6)

Wedgwood appears to be the only manufacturer to produce a Stilton cheese stand of this characteristic cylindrical shape as early as 1800, unless it is the lack of extant records which gives this impression. Adams were producing Jasper in competition with Wedgwood at the turn of the century but whether this included cheese stands is unknown. Unfortunately the records of the Adams' factory are very sparse and do not provide this information. It is probable, however, that if they produced any it may have been only a few before the late 1840s. As has already been mentioned it was the improvement in transportation of Stilton cheese in the late 1840s which stimulated demand for these Stilton cheese stands. Dudson, who also produced Jasperware from the early years of the 19th century, began producing these stands from this period.

Perhaps it might be useful at this point to make a very brief reference to the method of manufacture as the terms can be confusing to those who come new to the subject. The ware was made from a vitreous stoneware body which could be stained with metallic oxides (solid jasper) or it could be made in the white stoneware body which was then coloured, on the surface only, by dipping in a coloured slip (jasper dip). Small decorative motifs, formed in moulds (bas-reliefs or sprigs) were then applied by hand to the surface of the ware (sprigging).

The earliest producers, Wedgwood, Adams and Dudson were soon joined by Copeland and Ridgway. Although the demand began to increase from about 1850 it was not until the 1870s that

*Colour Plate 1* Dudson enamelled on relief over white glaze "Vertical Ferns."
Painted inside cover 3/9190 no other marks 1870/80. Height 28.75 cm.

*Colour Plate 2* Dudson - enamelled on relief "Hops, Vines & Wheat."
Painted number 4/1479 date impressed 6/72. Diameter 21.25 cm. Height 21.25 cm.

this market really flourished. From then, and throughout the 1880s, several manufacturers began to make jasper cheese stands. Many were of high quality but not all were marked.

It appears evident that every firm selling sprigged cheese stands produced classical decorations in the standard designs of Hunting (the Kill), Classical figures and/or Muses. (Colour Plates 7, 8, 9 & 10) Many of the sprigs were almost, or completely, identical leading to the possible conclusion that the moulds were purchased ex-works, from an independent modeller. Consequently it is difficult to determine the origin of manufacture unless the piece is marked. Fortunately Adams and Copeland normally impressed their ware and Ridgway fairly frequently. Wedgwood had a policy, from 1774, of always impressing all production lines. The odd piece would slip through but 99% of Wedgwood is clearly marked.[8] In 1860 Wedgwood began a system of three letter date codes on earthenware but only very occasionally does it occur on the Jasperware. Dudson did not impress on the base of the stands but sometimes, unfortunately not invariably, there is a hand written incised decoration number inside the dome. The characteristic rope knop is, however, often an aid to identification. The company's acorn knop, which was also used fairly frequently, is less easily identified with confidence as many other firms used acorn knops. Sometimes letters are impressed on Dudson pieces such as S. H. T. F. etc, especially W. These are workmen's marks but the W sometimes causes confusion as it is thought to stand for Wedgwood. Not so - it is the mark of one of Dudson's most skilled operatives.

Dudson began manufacturing in 1800 and is still privately owned, the firm being run today by the 7th and 8th generations in a direct, unbroken line from the founder. From 1850 onwards solid jasper cheese stands were produced in pale blue, light and dark brown and a greenish shade of turquoise stoneware. Jasper dip stands, so far recorded, include dark blue, light blue, a vibrant shade of mid-blue, pink, lavender, crimson and black, all on a white stoneware body. Like other manufacturers the classical

*(8) Miss Gaye Blake Roberts, Wedgwood Museum, Barlaston*

*Colour Plate 3* Unattributed - relief moulding of girl milking with embossed flowers enamelled. Unmarked 1870s. Height 20 cm.

*Colour Plate 4* Unattributed apple green slip dipped with white ribbons and fuschia - lightly gilded. There is a registration number but it is practically obscured by the glaze 1870-90. Height 22 cm.

*Colour Plate 5* Wedgwood blue slip dipped Stilton cheese stand with white bas-relief figures. Impressed WEDGWOOD c.1850. Diameter 25 cm.

*Colour Plate 6* Copeland dark blue slip dipped cheese stand with sprigged decoration. Impressed COPELAND 1850-90. Height 28.75 cm.

forms of decoration were used but Dudson is also noted for foliage sprigs, especially ferns of many varieties, birds and animals. The stands were produced in four sizes to take from the quarter up to the whole Stilton cheese.

It has already been stated that to make, and especially to fire, these large Stilton cheese stands required a special skill which Dudson obviously had. As a result other pottery factories occasionally purchased these dishes from Dudson and included them when supplying their own customers. The dishes were normal Dudson production lines but can be found with the other factory's name impressed on the base - a request included when ordering the dish. One factory to which this applied between the years 1872-82 was Brownhills Pottery Co (B. P. Co). After this date Brownhills - who were skilful potters - began to manufacture their own Jasperware and Dudson no longer supplied them. (Colour Plate 15) Further information on Dudson supplying other factories and on their range of sprig moulds and patterns is to be found in *Dudson - a Family of Potters since 1800*.[9]

Samuel Lear began potting in 1877 in a small works. In 1882 he expanded into new premises in High Street, Hanley where he produced quality jasper cheese stands. (Colour Plate 11) Fortunately they all appear to be impressed LEAR otherwise there would be considerable confusion between these and Dudson stands. Lear used the traditional classical decorations and, in all cases so far seen, the sprig moulds were identical to those used by Dudson. No evidence, however, exists to show that Dudson ever made Stilton cheese stands for Lear. It just underlines the difficulty of distinguishing between factories when they are applying the classical motifs. Unfortunately Samuel Lear went bankrupt in 1886. According to the Pottery Gazette of January 1887, *"considerable surprise has been excited over this bankrupt and his sudden disappearance has, to say the least of it, been a matter of much trade gossip."* His works were bought by Thomas Forester.

Another firm producing Jasperware cheese stands between

(9) *Audrey Dudson - Dudson Publications, 200 Scotia Road, Tunstall, Stoke on Trent 1985*

1873-86 was Adams & Bromley. Their cheese bells were truly bell shaped and two are illustrated in Colour Plates 10 & 22.

Demand for sprigged cheese stands started to decline during the late 1890s and by Edwardian times the main output was produced by Adams, Dudson and Wedgwood. Dudson had, by the 1890s, specialised in making hotelware i.e. special quality ware for the use of hotels and restaurants but prestige hotels throughout the world were still ordering the jasper cheese stands for the service of Stilton cheese.

Production ceased with the outbreak of war in 1914 - with one notable exception – Wedgwood. The early stand which Wedgwood introduced in 1800 had proved so popular that production continued throughout the 19th century, in two sizes. These were made in dark or pale blue jasper dip with white bas-reliefs of figures and oak border. In the 1870s a new bell-shaped round Stilton was introduced and featured in Wedgwood's Illustrated Catalogue of 1876. These were available in three sizes, in light or dark blue jasper dip with figures and oak border. Some years later an olive green dip was added. This round stand remains in production today and is currently supplied by Wedgwood, especially to Harrod's Ltd.

### Inlaid

This type of decoration was produced by running "rollers" or small roulette wheels round the unfired dome of the cheese stand thus impressing an intaglio design into the clay. This depression was then filled with a contrasting coloured slip which was allowed to dry. The cover, or dome, was then re-turned, smoothing the surface by removing the top layer and so revealing the pattern of alternating body and coloured slip.

Several factories employed this technique, especially Wedgwood, who made cheese stands decorated in this manner. However, examples from any factory are only infrequently seen on Stilton cheese stands at antiques fairs. The example illustrated in Plate 32 is by G L Ashworth & Bros Ltd (1862-80). (See page 43)

*Colour Plate* 7 Dudson dark blue slip dipped "Muses & Trees" incised 325 inside cover c.1850-90. Height 22.5 cm.

*Colour Plate* 8 Dudson dark blue slip dipped "Cherubs & Divisions" incised 1607. 1850-99. Height 27.5 cm.

*Colour Plate* 9 Unattributed dark blue slip dipped Stilton cheese stand unmarked c.1870-80. Height 20 cm.

*Colour Plate10* Adams & Bromley dark blue slip dipped with white classical figures unmarked but identified by the shape 1873-86. Height 27.5 cm.

*Fig 25* George Jones' Stilton cheese stands with polychrome underglaze prints 4393 and 4395 reproduced from an 1880 catalogue. (Courtesy Wedgwood Museum Trust)

*Fig 26* George Jones' polychrome print "Bullfinch on Apple Blossom" from an 1880 catalogue.

*Colour Plate 11* Samuel Lear bright blue slip dipped impressed LEAR 1877-86. Height 21.25 cm.

*Colour Plate 12* Copeland white stoneware Stilton cheese stand with dark brown bands and white sprigging impressed COPELAND 1850-90. Height 30 cm.

Inlaid "Mosaic" ware was also a speciality of the Dudson factory but only two cheese stands treated in this manner have so far been seen at antiques fairs. Both were produced in the 1870s in coloured stoneware body, one pale blue the other sage green, but regrettably, they were not photographed.

## Prints

Underglaze blue printing as a form of decoration on the early 19th century cheese stands has already been considered. Single colour printing remained popular for several decades until c.1850 but its popularity diminished when printing in several colours came into general use about that time. However there appears to have been a resurgence of popularity in the mid-1870s with what *Punch* magazine called "chinamania" i.e. a mania for collecting blue & white china. *Parents were said to love their china more than their children.* Blue and other single coloured prints were mainly applied to the new wedge shaped cheese dishes which matched dinner services of the period. Engraving a design to fit a specific shape such as a cheese bell was an expensive process and only employed when reasonable sales of that decoration could be expected. Large potteries such as Wedgwood who could employ their own engravers were producing printed Stilton stands from the late 1840s, but in the mid-1870s Dudson produced an underglaze blue print Stilton (Colour Plate 27) - perhaps in response to "chinamania".

From 1880 onwards polychrome prints were more popular. George Jones in particular produced some very attractive printed Stiltons which were illustrated in their 1880s catalogue - Fig 25 showing No 4393 has a cream background and brown handle, a spray of green leaves and red berries and a band of yellow or sometimes turquoise. No 4395 has a stylised pattern in blue, pink and old gold on a cream background. Figure 26 shows both sides of the pattern called "Bullfinch on Apple Blossom".

George Jones pieces are not always marked but frequently there is a monogram of the initials G J either above or below a crescent, and from 1873 onwards " & Sons" occurs in the crescent.

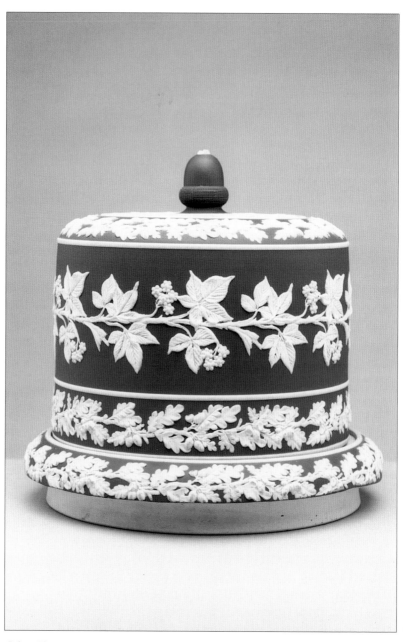

*Colour Plate 13* Dudson dark blue slip dipped "Blackberries" with "Oak" borders. Unmarked 1860-90. Height 27.5 cm. Also produced in pale lavender slip dip.

Sometimes however pieces which closely resemble George Jones' modelling and style of decoration but which are completely unmarked create a problem. Are they George Jones' unmarked pieces? Or were they in fact produced by another manufacturer because Jones' ware was popular and frequently imitated? Records of George Jones' production, which are held in the Wedgwood Museum at Barlaston, are unfortunately not very comprehensive for the 19th century so without further evidence, such as marked pieces turning up, either with the monogram or the design number, it is often exceedingly difficult to decide on an attribution. Colour Plates 24 & 25 illustrate this point.

**Jet Ware and Terracotta**
Another rather more expensive but very attractive form of printed decoration was the application of an outline print to terracotta or coloured stoneware body which was then over-painted with coloured enamels. The cheese stand in Plate 63 was produced at the Commondale factory near Stokesley in Yorkshire. The impressed mark "CROSSLEY COMMONDALE" was in use c.1872-90 but the firm ceased production of domestic earthenwares about 1884. They advertised cheese stands in buff or red terracotta, 10" and 12", highly ornamented in clay and enamelled. Characteristics of Commondale are naturalistic enamel decoration, usually white but also green, with dark brown enamelled lines and bands and also the particular shape of the acorn knop and moulded beading on either side of short radiating bands. Although the Stilton stand in Plate 43 is unmarked it could, for the above reasons, possibly be attributed to Commondale. (See page 50)

The Denby Pottery Co Ltd also advertised, in their catalogue of 1890 terracotta Stilton cheese stands, either plain or figured, which were available glazed or unglazed. However they are not illustrated. The Denby Pottery was founded by Joseph Bourne in 1809 at Denby in Derbyshire. Unfortunately no early shape books or catalogues are extant before this 1890 catalogue. Ware was often marked J Bourne & Son.

*Colour Plate 14* Dudson slate-blue stoneware full sized Stilton cheese stand "Hunting" incised 1335 inside the cover 1850-99. Height 30 cm.

*Colour Plate 15a* Dudson brown stoneware "Hunting" made for a special order from Brownhills Pottery Company incised 3376 inside cover impressed B P Co. Date impressed 827 (July 1882). Height 27.5 cm.

*Colour Plate 15b* Brownhills Pottery Company blue slip dipped half size Stilton cheese stand "Hunting" impressed B P Co ENGLAND date impressed 95 (1895). NB This dish was not made for them by Dudson.

*Colour Plate 16* Dudson light blue slip dipped "Cherubs" unmarked 1850-99. Height 27.5cm.

*Fig 27* Part of page 54 of the William Brownfield biscuit shape book, c.1876, which is in the Spode Archives at Keele University.

*Fig 28.* Page 98 from the William Brownfield biscuit shape book, c.1876, at Keele Universiry. (Courtesy Spode Ltd)

*Colour Plate 18* Dudson dark blue slip dipped "Allbine" incised 512 inside cover 1860-99.
Height 27.5 cm.

*Colour Plate 17* Dudson dark blue slip dipped "Festoon" unmarked 1850-99. Height 27.5 cm.

*Colour Plate 19* Dudson white stoneware with turned bands and white sprigs of bees scattered on surface, dark blue bands with white "Bryony" sprigging "Beehive". Missing base plate should have blue band with bees in white sprigging. Unmarked 1860-90. Height of cover only 22.5 cm. (Courtesy Harrod's Ltd)

*Plate 27* Dudson brown stoneware "Fern Wreath" incised 1253 inside cover impressed W 1860-99. Height 22.5 cm.

**Jet Ware**

Jet Ware was widely advertised in the 1870s/80s by many pottery firms although not all of them specified making cheese stands in this form and quality varied enormously. Some firms used "Jackfield" type glaze which was a very brilliant, high quality black glaze which can only be applied to a terracotta body. Others produced a cheaper version of this type of ware by using "Shiny-black" glaze on a white earthenware body which gave a somewhat inferior, less brilliant finish, the black colour being less intense. According to the descriptions given in the advertisements the cheapest versions were often left plain and only lightly gilded, but some had an attractive polychrome print applied to the ready glazed surface. Unfortunately few examples were illustrated.

Dudson produced Stilton cheese stands of this type but appears to have always used a terracotta body with Jackfield glaze. The cheese stand illustrated in Plate 44 has an orange print between two gold lines with borders of old gold print, lightly gilded, but Dudson also produced Jet cheese bells with outline transfers which were then hand-enamelled. The stand shown in Plate 45 is the "Cranes" pattern. The "Wild Flowers" pattern seen on the jug beside it was also used on Stilton cheese stands. These stands are generally unmarked except for, on occasion, a fractional number painted on the base or sometimes inside the dome, using one of the colours included in the decoration. Further details cannot be given as this system of marks has not yet been decoded. In spite of the many advertisements in the Pottery Gazette very few Jet Ware Stilton cheese stands are to be found in antiques fairs. (See pages 50 & 52)

**Majolica**

Majolica was the trade name for a typically Victorian ware made in the second half of the 19th century. It was Minton's Art Director, Leon Arnaux, who had the idea of reproducing the early 15th century Italian "Maiolica" and the ware was first introduced by Minton at the Great Exhibition of 1851 in London. The factory adopted the name "Imitation Majolica"

*Colour Plate 20* Dudson slate-blue stoneware "Fern & Bluebell" incised 418 inside cover date impressed 3.82 1860-99. Height 27.5 cm.

*Colour Plate 21* Dudson black slip dipped "Blackberries" with "Convolvulus" border unmarked 1860-90. Height 27.5 cm.

*Colour Plate 22* Adams & Bromley brown stoneware cheese stand impressed ADAMS & BROMLEY 1873-86. Height 21.25 cm.

*Colour Plate 23* Dudson dark brown stoneware "Vertical Ferns" incised 842 inside cover 1860-90. Height 30 cm.

*Colour Plate 24* Unmarked polychrome floral print on mauve background. Possibly attributable to George Jones but many firms closely followed his designs. c.1880. Diameter 27.5cm. Height 20 cm.

*Colour Plate 25* Unmarked polychrome floral print on blue ground (see Plate 57) c.1880. Diameter 27.5 cm. Height 30 cm.

*Colour Plate 26* Burgess & Leigh floral print on white - pattern name "Rename" printed mark (Godden 715) c.1870. Height 25 cm.

*Colour Plate 27* Dudson blue and white underglaze print lightly gilded. Date impressed 1.80 unmarked. Diameter 32 cm. Height 25 cm.

*Plate 28* Dudson brown stoneware "Birds
& Bamboo" unmarked 1860-90.
Height 22.5 cm.

*Plate 29* Dudson dark blue slip dipped
"Farm" unmarked 1850-90. Diameter
30.87 cm. Height 32.5 cm. There are other
variations of this stand, eg. with a vine
border top and bottom of the cover and
round base plate (incised 247) or with
stags and swans also included among the
animals.

*Plate 30* Dudson brown stoneware "Bird
& Butterfly" incised 3112 inside cover
1860-90. Diameter 12.25 cm. Height 25 cm.
This design was occasionally made for the
Brownhill's Pottery Company in which
case B P Co would also be impressed.

*Plate 31* Dudson light brown stoneware
"Fern Leaves" incised 787 inside cover.
Height 27.5 cm. It is interesting that this
fern has been identified at the Royal
Botanic Gardens, Kew as very precisely
copied from a natural specimen of
DORYOPTERIS ELEGANS.

because of the similarity to the Italian ware. However, similarity is the optimal word because although a few early pieces of Victorian Majolica were imitations of the 15th century Maiolica the vast majority were not. Within a few years the term Majolica meant earthenware decorated with coloured semi-translucent glazes. Victorian Majolica was usually made in an earthenware body, but occasionally in stoneware or Parian, and frequently the pieces were relief-moulded. They were then dipped into semi-translucent glazes, or painted with these same glazes to highlight parts of the moulding. Sometimes they were also gilded.

Minton's Majolica wares were soon copied by other manufacturers and Majolica was extremely popular by 1860. From then on throughout the 1870s it was produced by nearly every British pottery and competition was keen. By 1878 Minton was no longer pre-eminent and high quality competition was being provided by Wedgwood, George Jones, William Brownfield and others. Quoting from the *Pottery and Glass Trades' Review, June 1878:*

*"Judging from our experience we should say that Majolica ware is now the most popular class of decorated pottery. The taste for this class of wares appears to be rapidly on the increase and is spreading itself throughout every branch. Designs to suit majolica are in demand and everything in the way of novelty stands the best chance on the market of ultimate success. Of course a demand of this sort is not without its evil side which seems to be in sacrificing in many particulars good form to merely catchy. However we hope that the exuberance will sober down and that we shall have elegance as well as colour and that the chaste in design will be studied as well as the novel and surprising."*

Flamboyant the ware certainly was but it was also fun as can be seen by many of the Stilton cheese stands produced in this form. Nearly every type of ware imaginable was produced in Majolica, except dinner ware as the fragile nature of the glaze made it impractical, but amongst the most popular were the

*Plate 32* G L Ashworth Bros Ltd green stoneware cheese stand with black bands and inlaid decoration in white and yellow 1870-90.

*Plate 33* Davenport blue and white underglaze print. Printed mark c.1880. Diameter 22.5 cm Height 27.5 cm.

*Plate 35* George Jones' "Wild Rose" 6570 painted on base. Impressed monogram and crescent mark c1875-90. Diameter 32.5 cm. Height 27.5 cm.

*Plate 34* George Jones' "Apple Blossom" 3241 painted on the base. (Courtesy Harrod's Ltd)

*Plate 36* George Jones' "Seabirds" c.1880. Height 35 cm. (Courtesy Dr M Karmason)

*Plate 37* George Jones' "Calla Lily" No 5229 1870s-80s. Height 28.12 cm. (Courtesy Dr M Karmason) covered cheese dishes, especially the covered Stilton cheese stands which were often quite spectacular.

Around 1879 the Wedgwood factory appreciated the need for paler backgrounds and pastel coloured decorations, partly in answer to imported Continental production lines and partly because design was being influenced by Japanese art during the 1870s and 1880s.

People were beginning to tire of excessive flamboyance and to prefer more sober designs therefore white, cream and other pastel backgrounds increased in popularity although the deeper coloured grounds were still produced.

The Aesthetic Movement also exerted an influence on design during the 1880s with its opposition to flamboyance. The sunflower and the peacock, which were motifs of this movement, achieved great popularity.

The Majolica boom continued into the 1880s and put pressure on manufacturers so that quality was sometimes sacrificed to quantity. Many small firms decided to compete in this flourishing market and some of their products were poor quality indeed. This deterioration gradually led to a reduction in demand and by the 1890s Majolica was well past its prime.

## MAJOLICA MANUFACTURERS 1851 - 1890

### Minton

While Minton produced a wide range of beautiful Majolica Ware relatively few cheese stands were included in the range. They produced their "Ivy embossed" Stilton cheese stand c.1850 (Fig 16) and towards the end of the 1850s their "Mouse" cheese dish. (Fig 24) Both these shapes were included in the range of Majolica produced in the 1870s and early 1880s, but the earliest Majolica cheese stand which Minton exhibited was the "Beehive & Blackberry" at the 1862 London International Exhibition. This shape (page 58) was first made c.1860 and was still in production in 1884. It is included in the Minton 1884 catalogue along with shape 1461 and shape 546. (Fig 10) All three shapes continued in

*Plate 38* Thomas Forester pattern name unknown 1880-90. (Courtesy Dr M Karmason)

*Plate 39* Thomas Forester commemorative crown for the coronation of Edward VII registered in 1901 - registered No 380409. Diameter 25 cm. Height 20 cm.

production for many years and proved popular both in the original embossed form and later in Majolica.

Most Minton Majolica is impressed "Minton" or after 1873 "Mintons" and usually has a date cipher. It may also have the shape number on the plate.

## Wedgwood

The Wedgwood factory did not immediately compete with Minton in producing Majolica and it was not until c.1861 that they moved into this market. Even then it was in a modest way and their peak period did not come until 1876-80 when they introduced a total of 1300 lines although they continued to produce Majolica throughout the 1880s.

The extant Wedgwood Majolica pattern books[10]are the most extensive and complete of any pottery factory and provide much valuable information. Commencing in 1869 they continue until 1888 when entries cease. They show that from c.1869 onwards Wedgwood produced several Majolica cheese stands starting with two shapes, "Oak " and "Wicker" in the early part of the period.

(10) *Majolica pattern books belonging to J Wedgwood & Sons Ltd*
*M Majolica patterns 1869-76, 1876-88*
*K Majolica pattern book 1884*

*Plate 40* Wedgwood Majolica "Fan" impressed WEDGWOOD painted M2757 c.1876-90.

*Plate 41* Wedgwood Majolica "Palms" impressed WEDGWOOD W G H painted M2757. Diameter 22.8 cm c.1876-1890. (Courtesy City of Stoke-on-Trent Museum & Art Gallery)

47

## Oak

Oak was produced in various colour combinations. To give a few examples, other than that shown in Colour Plate 29, it was decorated with green leaves on either a blue or ivory background or with blue leaves on a stone ground. (See page 58)

## Wicker

There is no illustration of "Wicker" but the description in the pattern book (M1170) is *"centre panels grey, light orange bands and pink ties"*.

## Argenta

Around 1879 the Wedgwood factory introduced this new Majolica and named it "Argenta ware" - which simply means white background. This light background, which included ivory and other pastel shades, was excellent for the Japanesque designs, such as storks, fans and prunus blossom, which were so fashionable in the late 1870s and 80s. The first reference to Argenta ware as far as cheese stands are concerned is the "Cow Cheese Bell" M2698 recorded in the Wedgwood 1876-88 Majolica pattern book. (Colour Plate 41 Page 60)

For several reasons it has proved difficult, in spite of many enquiries, to obtain photographs of Wedgwood Majolica cheese stands. There are, fortunately, in the Wedgwood pattern books, original watercolour illustrations of some of their designs. Photography of these proved unsatisfactory so photocopies have been painted, by Helen Cooper, with watercolours carefully matched to the originals.[8a] These have been reproduced, so providing a special glimpse into early records not easily accessible to the majority of collectors. (See colour section pages 60 - 63)

## Wedgwood 1876 - 88

During this peak period the Wedgwood factory offered twelve Majolica Stilton cheese stands. "Oak", "Wicker" and "Cow" were still in production but nine new patterns were added.

*(8a) The helpfulness and co-operation of Miss Gaye Blake Roberts and the Wedgwood Museum Trust is gratefully acknowledged*

## Fan

This was the most popular Argenta pattern and was produced in six different colour combinations. (Plate 40)

## Primrose

Another popular pattern which was produced in seven colourways. (Colour Plate 42) Briefly, other colour combinations included yellow flowers on a mazerine blue or a brown background - or on a "dark white" background with silver leaves and pink berries. Another combination was blue and white flowers with dark blue leaves on a white background. It was also made in cane body.

## Palms

Another Argenta cheese stand with Japanesque decoration and elephant handle. (Plate 41 page 47) Three colour variations were available.

## New Matt

This was produced in three colour variations and also in cane body. (Colour Plate 43 page 61)

## Luther

This pattern appears for the first time in the Majolica K book 1884. It was made in two sizes "Low" and "Tall." Ten colour variations are listed which include such examples as Turquoise background with all ornament jade, and Jade background with all ornament gold and yellow.

There is an excellent watercolour illustration of K 3918 "background Ivory all ornament Turquoise" which is reproduced in Colour Plate 44.

## Chrysanthemum

Apparently also a popular pattern as it was produced in six colour combinations. It was made "Low" in cane body and "Tall" with Argenta, Ivory , Green or Crimson backgrounds.

There is a painting in the Wedgwood Majolica K book of

*Plate 42* Commondale terracotta cheese stand impressed CROSSLEY COMMONDALE across the footrim 1872-84. (Courtesy Mrs Crossley).

*Plate 43* Unattributed terracotta cheese stand. Possibly attributable to Commondale unmarked 1870s.

*Plate 44* Dudson Jackfield glazed terracotta cheese stand with on glaze matt orange transfer gilded unmarked 1870s-80s. Height 25cm.

pattern K3794, the "Low" version in cane body. This has been reproduced in Colour Plate 45.

There are no illustrations for the "Tall" version but quoting from one description gives some indications:

K3526  Background green
     Downward stripes and stems - brown
     Leaves - yellow green
     Icicles on top of knop - green
     Band under knop and over flowers - brown
     Flowers alternately yellow and white

Two further Majolica designs introduced in the early 1880s were "Flemish" and "Lincoln". There are no illustrations for either.


## Flemish ( M3445 & M3446)

This was produced in two sizes:-

a) Tall  Background citron yellow
     chrysanthemum flowers in mixed crimson and
     brown.
b) Small  White background
     crimson chrysanthemums with brown centres.

This is obviously very similar to "Chrysanthemum". Both have icicles on top of the knop but "Flemish" does not have the stripes down the bell.

## Lincoln (M3425 & M3425)

This was produced with a white glazed background and olive green leaves. Flowers, unspecified, are decorated in either of two ways:

a) Pink with a yellow centre which has brown bamboo and a citron handle.
b) Citron flowers shaded with pink, olive green bamboo and a brown handle.

*Plate 45* Dudson Jackfield glazed terracotta cheese stand printed and hand enamelled "Cranes" 1870s. Height 27.5 cm. The jug is decorated with "Wild Flowers" which was also used on Dudson cheese stands.

*Plate 46* Unattributed earthenware cheese stand with a polychrome print applied over a "shiny black" glaze unmarked 1870s-80s.

## Ansty

Wedgwood also produced a plain Stilton cheese bell and stand in two sizes - tall and small - sometimes given a Majolica glaze. (Fig 14 page 14)

Most Wedgwood Majolica is impressed WEDGWOOD. In 1860 Wedgwood began a system of date coding which consists of three letters - charts can be found in most books of marks - and sometimes also the pattern number is painted on the base plate prefixed by M or K.

## George Jones

George Jones, like Minton and Wedgwood, produced very high quality Majolica. He was trained at Minton but started his own factory in 1861 and towards the end of the 1860s he was an established manufacturer, especially of Majolica. The firm remained in business for 90 years before closing in 1951. There is, unfortunately, very little information available about the products apart from a Majolica shape book and parts of a catalogue, both relating to the 1880s, which are in the Wedgwood archives together with an Illustrated Price List of 1873.

The following Majolica Stilton cheese bells are recorded in the Illustrated Price List of 1873. Prices at which they were sold make an interesting comparison with those of today.

| | | | |
|---|---|---|---|
| 2586 | "Goat" | Stilton cheese bell made in full size only | 16/- (80p) |
| 3279 | "Beehive" | Only the half size cheese bell was produced in Majolica | 15/6 (78p) |
| | | The full size was produced in white glaze only. | 9/- (45p) |
| 3240 | "Apple Blossom" | | |
| | | Full size Majolica | 12/6 (63p) |
| 3241 | | Half size Majolica | 10/- (50p) |
| | | matching base plate | 7/6 (38p) |
| 2683 | "Apple Blossom" | | |
| | | White glaze with coloured leaves, blossoms and handles | |

|  |  |  |  |
|---|---|---|---|
|  | Full size |  | 10/6 (53p) |
|  | Half size |  | 9/- (45p) |
|  | matching white glazed plate |  | 6/6 (33p) |
| 2665 "Apple Blossom" |  |  |  |
|  | coloured with gold line |  |  |
|  | Full size |  | 12/6 (63p) |
|  | Half size |  | 10/6 (53p) |
|  | matching plate |  | 8/- (40p) |
| 3341 "Tower" | Majolica |  | 10/6 |
|  | white glaze |  | 6/6 |
|  | white glaze & gold |  | 10/6 |
| 2200 "Cow" | Majolica | Full | 12/- |
|  |  | Half | 9/6 |
|  | white glaze | Full | 7/- |
|  |  | Half | 6/- |
|  | white with gold lines |  |  |
|  |  | Full | 12/- |
|  |  | Half | 11/- |
| 1750 "Rustic" | Majolica | Full | 10/- |
|  |  | Half | 8/6 |
|  |  | 3rd size | 6/9 |
|  | white glaze | Full | 13/- |
|  |  | Half | 11/6 |
|  |  | 3rd size | 9/6 |
| 1941 "Rustic" | white, gold & coloured |  |  |
|  |  | Full | 14/- |
|  |  | Half | 12/6 |
|  |  | 3rd size | 10/6 |
| 2649 "Rustic" | white glaze, coloured |  |  |
|  |  | Full | 10/- |
|  | but no gilding | Half | 8/6 |

All the above cheese stands were registered. The colouring, on white glaze, was done with semi-translucent coloured glazes to highlight parts of the relief moulding. (Colour Plate 28 page 57)

The George Jones pattern book of 1880 has an illustration of

"Wild Rose on brown" (3573) which is reproduced in Colour Plate 46 (see also Plate 35). A third version (6573) is also described as red and gold on an ivory ground. There are two further illustrations in this 1880 pattern book: "Daisy" (5204) and "Lotus" (3484) which are reproduced in Colour Plates 47 & 48. Once again watercolours matching the originals of these three patterns have been painted by Helen Cooper by kind permission of the Wedgwood Museum Trust. (See colour section pages 60 - 63).

George Jones' Stilton cheese stands are much admired and sought after but patterns were frequently imitated or adapted by potteries on both sides of the Atlantic so care must be taken when identifying. Fortunately the factory frequently marked their Majolica with impressed monograms of the letters G J and some unmarked pieces can be identified by the pattern number if it is painted on the base.

### W T Copeland & Sons
Copeland produced a wide range of Majolica ware which included the "Caltha" and "Rutland" cheese stands. (Figs 21 & 22) These were first introduced in the 1860s and were still in production in the 1880s in stoneware, Parian and Majolica glazed.

The Copeland factory was meticulous about marking ware by impressing COPELAND on the base but in the case of Majolica the glaze sometimes obscures it.

### William Brownfield & Co
The Brownfield company exhibited Majolica at the London Exhibition of 1871.

In the Spode Archives at Keele University Library there is a Brownfield shape book which consists of sepia photographs of wares in the bisque state. This includes four Stilton cheese bells which are known to have been made in Majolica: "Maple", "Chestnut", "Tower" and "Bamboo". The book is rather stained and damaged in places so, regrettably, does not reproduce very clearly, however it gives some indication of the designs (Fig 27, 28 page 36) See also plates 20 and 21. (page 22).

More Stilton cheese stands are illustrated on page 98 of the same book but there is no indication as to whether these were produced in Majolica or not. (Fig 28 page 36)

## Thomas Forester

Thomas Forester commenced potting in 1877 and was established at the Phoenix works, Longton by c.1880 when his business was described as quite extensive. An advertisement in the Pottery Gazette 1st February 1883 mentions "Stork" Stilton cheese stands made in five sizes (Colour Plate 33). Another article in the Crockery and Glass Journal 19th October 1882 refers to three more of his Stilton cheese stands: "Ribbon", "Berry" and "Hawthorn." Plate 38 and 39 illustrate two of Thomas Forrester's cheese stands and it is possible that Colour Plate 34 could be the design called "Ribbon."

Forester continued to produce Majolica later than most other firms and registered this cheese stand (Plate 39 page 46) presumably as a commemorative piece for the coronation of Edward VII.

Thomas Forester did not always mark his ware but it may have a printed or impressed mark T F & S.

## Joseph Holdcroft

Joseph Holdcroft worked at Minton for eighteen years before starting up on his own in 1875. For two years he potted at St Martin's Lane, Longton but in 1877 he moved to the Sutherland works also in Longton where he made lustre and Parian but mainly Majolica. (Colour Plates 35 & 36) Holdcroft sometimes impressed his name or a monogram of J H.

## Samuel Lear

Samuel Lear began potting c.1877 at the Mayer Street works in Hanley. This factory was very small but in 1882 expanded into new premises in High Street, Hanley, where Ivory, Jasperware and Majolica were produced. (Colour Plate 37)

*Colour Plate 28* Page from George Jones pattern book c.1873 showing "Goat" (2586), "Beehive" (3279), "Apple Blossom" (3240), "Tower" (3341), "Cow" (2200) and "Rustic" (1750). (Courtesy Wedgwood Museum Trust)

*Colour Plate 29* Minton Majolica shape No 969 "Beehive & Blackberry" c.1860-80s. Height 32.5 cm.

*Colour* Plate 30 Wedgwood Majolica cheese stand "Oak" impressed WEDGWOOD 1870-c1890. Height 17.5 cm (M2196).

*Colour Plate 31* George Jones' impressed mark and registration mark c.1870-80s. Diameter 27 cm. Height 35 cm.

*Colour Plate 32* George Jones' "Wild Strawberry" impressed monogram G J c.1870-90.

*Colour Plate 34* Thomas Forester pattern name unknown 1880s.
(Courtesy Dr M Karmason)

*Colour Plate 33* Thomas Forester "Stork" 1880s. Height 30 cm. (Courtesy Dr M Karmason)

*Colour Plate 35* J Holdcroft impressed HOLDCROFT c.1880. Height 20 cm. (Courtesy Dr M Karmason)

*Colour Plate 36* J Holdcroft "Bramble" impressed HOLDCROFT c.1880. Base diameter 29 cm. (Courtesy Dr M Karmason)

*Colour Plate 37* S Lear impressed LEAR 1882-86. Height 20.6 cm.

*Colour Plate 38* W & J A Bailey ALLOA impressed mark c.1881-83. Height 30.6 cm.

*Colour Plate 39* Robinson, Leadbetter & Leason "Victoria" cheese stand impressed VICTORIA POTTERY CO 1882-83. Height 27.5 cm.

*Colour Plate 40* Griffen, Smith & Hill 1870-80. (Courtesy Dr M Karmason)

*Colour Plate 41* Wedgwood "Cow" cheese bell pattern M2698. Reproduction of painting in Majolica pattern book 1869-76. (Courtesy Wedgwood Museum Trust)

*Colour Plate 42* Wedgwood "Primrose" cheese bell pattern M1744. Reproduced from Majolica pattern book 1876-88.

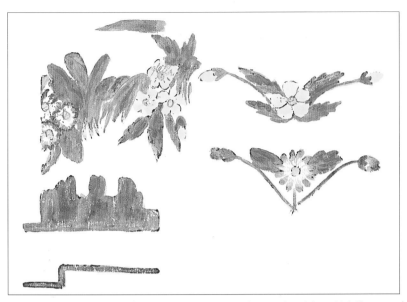

*Colour Plate 43* Wedgwood "New Matt" pattern M2905. Reproduced from Majolica pattern book 1876-88.

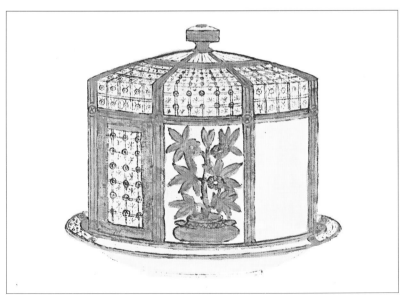

*Colour Plate 44* Wedgwood "Luther" cheese bell pattern K3918. Reproduced from Majolica K book 1884.

*Colour Plate 45* Wedgwood "Chrysanthemum" cheese bell pattern K3794. Low cheese stand also made in cane body. Reproduced from Majolica K book 1884.

*Colour Plate 46* George Jones "Wild Rose" on brown (Pattern 3573). Reproduced from 1880 pattern book. (Courtesy the Wedgwood Museum Trust)

*Colour Plate 47* George Jones "Daisy" (Pattern 5206). Reproduced from George Jones'
1880 pattern book. (Courtesy Wedgwood Museum Trust)

*Colour Plate 48* George Jones "Lotus" (Pattern 3484). Reproduced from George Jones'
1880 pattern book. (Courtesy Wedgwood Museum Trust)

## W & J A Bailey c.1855 - 1908

This firm potted at the Alloa pottery in Fife, Scotland and through 1881 - 1883 they advertised Majolica ware in flower pots, dessert ware, teapots, kettles, jugs and cheese stands and covers. (Colour Plate 38) They sometimes impressed their Majolica ware W & J A BAILEY, ALLOA.

## Robinson, Leadbetter & Leason

This firm was of very short duration. Opening at the Victoria Pottery in Stoke in 1882 but not appearing to advertise after 1883. An article in the *Crockery and Glass Journal 10th August 1882* gives a description of their "Victoria" cheese stand as:

> *"made in three sizes......a novel design of a combination of bamboo, canes and foliage with a ground work of rushes skilfully interlaced....... the background of rushes in dull brown throws up in relief the cane colour of bamboo and foliage, the rushes being treated in a most natural manner showing the joining where new rushes have been inserted or where the rushes have split under the weavers' fingers."*

This design was registered, by whom it is not known, but Victoria Bergesen in her *"MAJOLICA"* book (page 157) tells us it was not registered by Robinson, Leadbetter and Leason (nor by Robinson and Leadbetter a different company who specialised in Parian). (Colour Plate 39)

Many other pottery factories produced Majolica cheese stands as can be seen from a study of advertisements in the *Pottery Gazettes* of the 1880s. Few included illustrations and information from other sources is not easily obtainable. Victoria Bergesen gives very comprehensive coverage to Majolica manufacturers - both British and American - in her *"MAJOLICA"* book, as does Marilyn Kermason in her book on *"Majolica"*, both books are recommended to Majolica collectors although they are not, of course, specific to cheese stands.

Colour Plate 40 shows a particularly attractive Stilton dish of American manufacture - by Griffen, Smith & Hill of Pennsylvania, the best known American Majolica manufacturer.

# 5

# LATE 19TH CENTURY WEDGE SHAPED CHEESE DISHES

W hile cheese stands continued in popularity to the end of the century, in the 1860s a demand was created for a small, covered cheese dish. This was brought about by a change in the social customs of the newly emancipated Victorian middle class. They were influenced by *"The Englishwoman's Domestic Magazine"* which was launched in 1852 with Samuel Beeton as its editor; its circulation exceeded all expectations. After his marriage in 1856 his wife Isabella gradually took over the proof reading, began to write articles for it and finally took almost complete control. In 1859 she brought out a separate supplement to the magazine dealing entirely with cookery and domestic matters. This became so popular that the twenty-four monthly issues were published as a single volume.[6] Doubtless other factors played a part too, but Mrs Beeton told her readers *"Dinner without cheese is like a woman with one eye"* and so it became fashionable to introduce a cheese course to be eaten between pudding and dessert.

*2101*

*Cheese Stand*

*Fig 45* Wedgwood footed cheese dish introduced during the 1870s - shape 2101 in cream coloured earthenware 10" (25 cm), 11" (27.5 cm) & 12" (30 cm) in all decorations to match dinner ware. From Wedgwood catalogue of shapes 1880. (Courtesy Wedgwood Museum Trust)

In the early 1860s it was usual to serve cheese cut into neat squares which were handed round in a glass dish or on a footed pottery dish. The latter were still being produced by various factories; indeed Wedgwood discontinued their earlier shapes (Fig 5) and introduced a new one. (Fig 45) However some varieties of cheese were too crumbly for this treatment, which led to waste and a less attractive appearance, so sometimes it was desirable to serve the cheese in the piece.

At the same time a suggestion became widely accepted that all cheese, and not only Stilton, would be better served covered. It was the custom to cover Stilton to prevent the smell pervading the room, but soon it was realised that aroma from all cheeses added to the pleasure of eating them. This led to the production of small covered cheese dishes to conserve the aroma of other varieties and to prevent the cheese drying.

As the cheese course became more popular manufacturers began offering cheese dishes as a matching part of dinner services and by the 1870s this was normal procedure. It is easy therefore, to imagine what vast numbers of cheese dishes were produced when one thinks of all the pottery factories and the great number of dinner services each one sold. Many of them did not mark their ware, and alas, records no longer exist for the majority of these factories, which explains why there are so many pretty wedge shaped cheese dishes for which it is quite impossible to establish the maker.

Service of cheese was not, of course, restricted to formal entertaining but constituted an important part of the daily diet. Many varieties were available from a large selection of local cheeses to several expensive imported ones. To meet the increased demand at a more reasonable cost cheese factories were introduced in the 1870s producing, especially, the favourites of Cheshire, Cheddar, Leicester and Stilton. Consequently it is not surprising that production of cheese dishes also accelerated throughout the 1870s. Dishes continued to be included in dinner services but increasingly dishes with other forms of decoration were designed to be sold separately. For example Wedgwood introduced a new shape (Fig 46) and added a wedge shaped dish to their Lavender Ware range.

Before considering these new shapes of dishes this might be the time to point out that all cheese dishes have a hole, or holes, in the cover to discourage mould from forming. If holes are not present the dish is more probably a butter dish or, if oblong, a sardine dish.

*Fig 46* Wedgwood wedge shaped cheese dish shape C 3670 - decorated to match various dinner services c.1870 onwards. (Wedgwood Museum Trust)

## BASIC SHAPES

The wedge shape easily predominated but other basic shapes were introduced. Although smaller than a Stilton cheese stand all shapes were, nevertheless, fairly large - after all the Victorians did not have small families.

### Wedge

Although made to take a wedge shaped piece of cheese, the majority of these dishes were prettily curved but towards the end of the century some dishes became more angular and manufacturers sometimes substituted Desk shape for wedge shape.

The dish shown in Colour Plate 50 was registered in March 1869 but cannot be attributed as no manufacturer's name was recorded in the Public Records Office, London, for this registration number. However, it is interesting to compare it with the dish in Colour Plate 51 which was produced by William Alsager Adderley (1886-1905).

*Colour Plate 49* Burgess & Leigh Reg. No 221859 registered 1868 unmarked except for impressed 2, still in production in the 20th C (see plate 85) 1868-c1930.

*Colour Plate 50* Unattributed - registered March 1869 but factory name not recorded.

*Colour Plate 51* Similar shape to 90a. William Alsager Adderley printed mark (Godden 49) and W A & Co 1886-1905.

## Semi-Circular Segment

*Fig 47* Minton semi-circular segment reproduced from Minton shape book c.1879. Height 21.25 cm. Length 26.25 cm.

## Tent

*Fig 48* Copeland "Chelsea" tent shape from the 1880s catalogue but first introduced c.1870s. (Courtesy Spode Museum Trust)

## Triangular

Colour Plate 54 shows a shape, which was registered in 1887 by an un-named factory, with two quite different decorative treatments. S Fielding & Co produced a triangular cheese dish in the 1890s with flower sprays, printed on the sides, such as "poppy", "chrysanthemum" etc. Plate 55 may have been made by that firm. The handle, position of the flower spray and the gilding all match their advertisements in the *Pottery Gazette* in the 1890s, but the base plate is not identical. (Colour Plate 55)

Brownhill's Pottery Company produced a triangular cheese dish in their well-known Japanese bamboo pattern in the 1880s/90s.

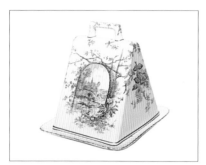

*Colour Plate 52* Edge Malkin tent shape. Reg. No 49583 printed mark E M & Co 1886/87. Height 22.5 cm. Width 20 cm. Length 22.5 cm.

*Colour Plate 53* Powell, Bishop & Stonier tent shape, pattern name "Lichfield" printed along with P B & S (Godden 3137) 1879-91.

*Colour Plate 54* Two unattributed triangular shaped dishes. Reg. No 78542 1887.

*Colour Plate 55* Unattributed "Rose" triangular cheese dish 1890s.

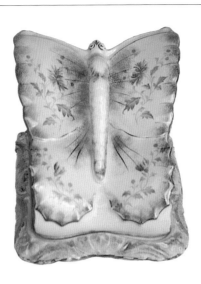

*Colour Plate 56* Unattributed cheese dish modelled as a butterfly unmarked.
Height 15 cm. Length 22.5 cm. c.1870-1890. Note that Blakeney Art Pottery are
producing a similarly modelled butterfly cheese dish in their Flow Blue Victoria Ware -
in current production from 1968 clearly marked with a Blakeney backstamp.

*Colour Plate 57* Wedgwood "S" line cheese dish. Impressed WEDGWOOD painted inside
the dome S253 c.1900. Height 20 cm. (Courtesy Mr C R Portess)

*Colour Plate 58* Grimwade Brothers advertisement of 1888 from the Pottery Gazette October 1st 1888. (Courtesy Gladstone Pottery Museum)

*Plate 47* Brownhills Pottery Co horseshoe shape, pattern name "Filbert" printed over a leaf. Impressed B P Co ENGLAND 1891-96.

*Plate 48* Unattributed horseshoe shape.

## Square

The cheese dish in Plate 73 is unmarked but this pattern of outline-printed peonies in red with cobalt blue leaves occurs on the rim of plates which have a Chinese scene in the centre. These plates are stamped Mason's Ironstone China and impressed Mason's Ironstone China. There is, however, no further evidence to establish this cheese dish as Mason. (Page 87)

## Oval

Plate 74, page 87.

## Horseshoe Shape

Plate 47

Plate 48

## Round

Relatively few small round cheese dishes appear to have been designed in the 1880s/90s and the two illustrated are of unknown manufacture. (Plates 51 & 52 page 78)

Some manufacturers, however, reduced the size of models already in their production. Copeland did this with their Chelsea shape (Fig 23) and Dudson produced a much smaller version of their design Fern Wreath than the four sizes of Stiltons previously produced. The round shape acquired greater popularity a few years later. (Plate 49)

The increased production of the 1870s led to the peak period of thirty years from the early 1880s up to the First World War. This coincided, in the 1890s, with a steady decline in the production of the large cheese bells as the fashion for purchasing whole, or circular sections, of Stilton cheese gave way to a preference for wedge shaped portions. Consequently many firms produced extra large wedge shaped dishes, which they advertised as "Desk Stiltons" or triangular ones as "Wedge Stiltons." Dudson introduced a new half-moon shaped Stilton. (Plate 50)

The output of cheese dishes was vast but one firm's production seems to have been so prolific that it warrants special

*Plate 49* Dudson slate-blue stoneware "Fern Wreath" incised inside the cover 998 unmarked. 1870-90. Diameter 18.75 cm. Height 12.5 cm.

*Plate 50* Dudson half-moon shaped cheese dish - introduced 1898 "Muses & Trees." Impressed DUDSON ENGLAND. 1898-c1914. Height 16.25 cm. Width 22.5 cm. Length 25 cm.

*Fig 50* Grimwades Ltd advertisement 1906.

mention. From 1886, when the firm of Grimwade Brothers was established, they produced inexpensive wedge shaped cheese dishes with lithographed designs, i.e. multi-coloured prints applied in one operation, and their advertisements stress "immense variety" and similar phrases. In the *Pottery Gazette* during 1888 they inform that their lithograph designs are sold in suites which include *"jugs and jug stand, teapot, coffee pot, bacon dish, sardine dish, bread tray and wedge cheese dish"*. Colour Plate 58 illustrates the various items and presumably cheese dishes were produced in all these designs. (page 72)

In 1900 the name of the firm changed to Grimwades Ltd and they continued to produce light-weight earthenware cheese dishes, with coloured prints, very cheaply. (Fig 50) Their dishes normally have printed marks and these are very comprehensively covered in Geoffrey Godden's *Encyclopedia of British Pottery and Porcelain Marks* but briefly they have the initials G B, or in 1900, Stoke pottery under a crown, or maybe WINTON or RUBIAN ART if they do not have the whole name. Often Grimwade shapes include "Fluted", "Concave" and "Hawthorn" to name but a few.

The following are examples from advertisements in the Pottery Gazette.

*Fig 51* Grimwade Brothers three 1890s shapes: a) "Fleur de Saxe" fluted shape assorted colours. b) "Hawthorn" wedge enamelled in bright colours. c) "Concave" wedge enamelled in bright colours.

*Fig 52* Hines Brothers, Stoke-on-Trent "Ionic" shape Reg. No 128494 "Orchid" enamelled and gilded. Also a variety of other patterns on this shape usually impressed H B 1892.

*Plate 51* Unattributed round cheese dish with flower print on white glaze. C or crescent printed on the base. c.1900. Height 12.5 cm. Width 25 cm.

*Plate 52* Unattributed round cheese dish with orange print. Impressed 04 painted 222 c.1900. Height 12.5 cm.

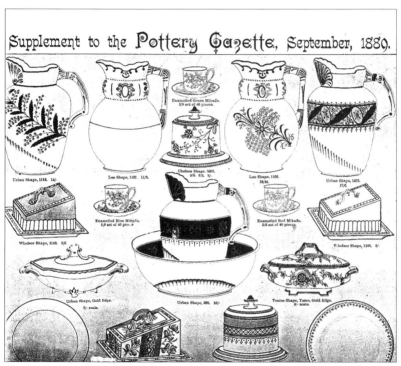

*Fig 53* John Tams "Windsor" shape wedge and "Chelsea" shape Stilton cheese stand made in three sizes 1889. Marked J T or J Tams in printed marks.

*Fig 54* Sampson Hancock, Bridge Works. Two desk shaped cheese dishes.
a & b Numbers 651 and 648. Fluted and enamelled in various patterns. S H found on
various printed marks name of the pattern is often included 1889.

## GERMAN CHEESE DISHES 1890 - 1920s

Cheese dishes were also popular production lines from some continental factories, especially German, and some of their ware naturally found its way into Britain. Special mention should be made of two German potteries at Bonn in the Rhineland as examples of their cheese dishes are readily available here, namely Franz A Mehlem 1755-, and Popplesdorf which was owned by Ludwig Wessel 1825-. Both usually have printed marks. Those by Franz A Mehlem generally incorporate an anagram of the letters F A M, whilst those of Ludwig Wessel contain the letters L W P or the full word of Popplesdorf, as the examples shown here.

Comprehensive coverage of continental marks, especially German, are to be found in the *Handbook of Pottery & Porcelain Marks* by J P Cushion.

*Plate 53* Franz A Mehlem fluted cheese dish - printed mark c.1890.

*Plate 54* Franz A Mehlem - printed mark c.1890.

*Plate 55* Franz A Mehlem - printed mark c.1880-1890.

*Plate 56* Franz A Mehlem scuttle shaped cheese dish - printed mark c.1890.

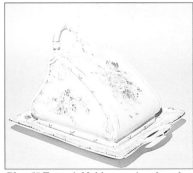

*Plate 57* Franz A Mehlem - printed mark c.1900.

*Plate 58* Popplesdorf - printed mark c.1890-1920.

*Plate 59* Popplesdorf - printed mark c.1900.

*Plate 60* Charles Barlow, Smithfield Works, Hanley, Staffordshire, printed mark
CHARLES BARLOW - a lion and unicorn under a crown with underneath BY ROYAL
LETTERS PATENT. Presumably this refers to a method of ornamenting pottery with
bright and dull gold which was patented in October 1882.

*Plate 61* Keeling & Co Ltd "Tokio" printed mark (Godden 2243) c.1890-1910. (Courtesy Hornsea Museum)

*Plate 62* Keeling & Co Ltd 1419 printed mark (Godden 2243) c.1890-1910. (Courtesy Hornsea Museum)

*Plate 63* Wiltshaw & Robinson Carlton
Ware "Catalpa" Reg. No 213522 printed
mark (Godden 4201) 1894-1900. Height
12.5 cm. Width 20 cm. Length 25 cm.

*Plate 64* Burgess & Leigh pattern name
"Rustic" printed Hill Pottery mark
(Godden 715) c.1870-89.

*Plate 65* Ridgways' pattern name
"Carlton" printed mark (Godden 3312)
c.1905-20.

*Plate 66* Boulton, Machin & Tennant
printed mark (Godden 469) 1890s. Height
10 cm. Width 16.25 cm. Length 21.25 cm.

Plate 67 Three identical cheese dishes all of which have the same printed mark of a lion to the left and a unicorn to the right under a crown (as Plate 113 but without other marks)

Plate 68 William Adams printed mark W ADAMS & Co SEMI-PORCELAIN 1880-1900.

Plate 69 F Winkle & Co impressed F W & Co STOKE 1890-1910.

Plate 70 Unattributed triangular or desk shaped cheese dish with underglaze blue print c 1880-1890.

*Plate 71* Unmarked but was professionally identified as Mason Ironstone china manufactured by G L Ashworth Ltd c.1890.

*Plate 72* Unattributed pattern name "Orient" impressed and also an impressed device which was not identifiable c.1890.

*Plate 73* Unattributed square shaped cheese dish.

*Plate 74* Unattributed oval cheese dish - orange and yellow flowers.

*Plate 75* Unattributed but unusually shaped cheese dish embossed and enamelled c 1870-1880s.

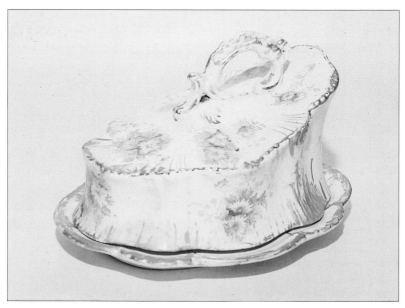

*Plate 76* Unidentified cheese dish c 1890.

# 6

# THE EARLY 20TH CENTURY

The early years of the 20th century saw an influx of wedge shaped cheese dishes, some still matching dinner services but, increasingly, more novel, individual examples were designed. Very decorative ornamentation continued in popularity influenced by the flowing, rather florid Art Nouveau style which had been introduced on the Continent at the close of the 19th century. This style lasted up to the outbreak of the First World War in 1914 when changes were initiated. During the war cheese production was restricted and the Depression which followed also influenced the purchase of cheese, consequently cheese dishes were made much smaller than previously. Public taste also changed and the geometric, angular lines of Art Deco in the 1920s resulted in simpler shapes and bright colours being preferred.

With the outbreak of the Second World War, in September 1939, demand for cheese dishes was greatly reduced - the small cheese ration looked even smaller if put onto a cheese dish - but in addition production ceased too. The Limitation of Supply Act prevented manufacture of this type of ware for the home market. Only Utility ware, i.e. plain white ware in very few shapes, was permitted so as to discourage the public from buying anything that was not strictly essential. This helped to free much of the pottery workforce to serve in the armed services. Small amounts of decorated ware were produced by a limited number of potters for sale on the export market only.

To return, however, to the beginning of the century, the largest producer was undoubtedly Royal Doulton with their attractive Series Ware.

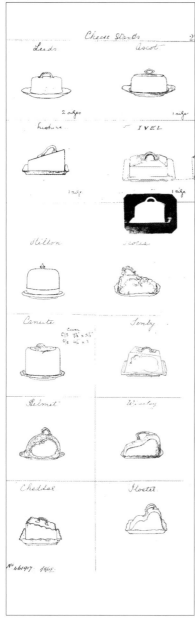

Fig 56 Royal Doulton design D/N 2507 on "Cheddar" shape from the Doulton 1905 catalogue.

Fig 57 Royal Doulton design D/N 2570 on "Canute" shape from the Doulton 1905 catalogue.

Fig 55 Pages 21/22 from the Royal Doulton shape book dated 9.2.33 but the shapes were registered in 1905. (Courtesy Royal Doulton Ltd)

Fig 58 Royal Doulton "Countess" design D/N 2802 on "Leeds" shape from the 1923-29 catalogue.(Courtesy Royal Doulton Ltd)

## Royal Doulton Ltd

Utility wares were being produced by Henry Doulton in his Lambeth works towards the end of the 1850s. In the early 1860s he added some decorated stoneware and earthenware to his range and it is known that the range included salt glazed brown cheese stands.

A partnership with Pinder Bourne & Co in Nile Street, Burslem, Stoke-on-Trent was entered into in 1877 with Doulton acquiring sole ownership in 1882 and here the firm produced tableware and ornamental ware. Production at this works was to include many smaller cheese dishes throughout the years to come.

Exactly when the production of cheese dishes began is not certain but the archives show that in 1898 Doulton introduced design A/K9627 on their "Helmet" shape and this appears to be one of the earliest. It was certainly the first of a very extensive range of designs produced on the following shapes which were registered by Doulton 1st August 1905 (Fig 55). Like Helmet some of these shapes were in production prior to registration. (Plate 77)

The following list gives some indication as to how extensive is the range of designs by Doulton. This list is not complete. The dates of introduction are by Louise Irvine and are taken from her *"Royal Doulton Series Ware."* There are four volumes and collectors are recommended to this series for illustrations of the designs. An index is to be found at the back of Volume 4.

Some Doulton Pattern Numbers with their date of Introduction:

| | | |
|------|------------------|------|
| D 653 | Blue Willow | 1900 |
| D2654 | Churches | 1906 |
| D2538 | Frieze | 1906 |
| D2652 | Norfolk | 1906 |
| D2532 | Jackdaw of Rheims | 1906 |
| D2716 | Coaching | 1906 |
| D2780 | Terriers | 1907 |
| D2872 | Ships | 1907 |
| D2735 | No name | 1907 |

| D2973 | Dickens | 1908 |
|--------|---------|------|
| D3191 | Gleaners | 1909 |
| D3368 | Burn's Subjects | 1910 |
| D3302 | Greek Figures | 1910 |
| D3382 | Willow | 1911 |
| D3416 | Poplars and Sunset | 1911 |
| D3419 | Egyptian | 1911 |
| D3395 | Golf | 1911 |
| D3418 | Sir Roger | 1911 |
| D3596 | Shakespeare | 1912 |
| D3538 | Tunis | 1912 |
| D3680 | Gallant Fishers | 1913 |
| D3668 | Landscape | 1913 |
| D3696 | Falconry | 1913 |
| D3647 | Countryside | 1913 |
| D3749 | Peter Pan | 1914 |
| D3811 | Wattle Frieze | 1914 |
| D3751 | Robin Hood | 1914 |
| D3754 | The Open Door | 1914 |
| D3812 | Blue Bells | 1914 |
| D3832-3 | Prunus | 1915 |
| D3858 | Old Moreton Hall | 1915 |
| D4049 | Pansies | 1916-18 |
| D4031 | Blue Persian | 1916-18 |
| D4149 | Shakespeare's Country | 1921-22 |
| D4222 | Bird of Paradise | 1921-22 |
| D4210 | Gaffers | 1921-22 |
| D4251-2 | Anemones | 1923 |
| D4243 | Minstrels | 1923 |
| D4390 | Landscape | 1924 |

A most unusual Doulton cheese dish is illustrated on Plates 78-80. The cover is in two sections - one lower than the other. They are attached by the knop passing through both sections. To open the cheese dish the lower dish revolves underneath the higher section.

All Doulton cheese stands have the Doulton mark.

*Plate 77* Royal Doulton cheese dish "Old Leeds" spray on "Cheshire" shape. Standard impressed mark 1900-1930. (Courtesy Hornsea Museum)

*Plate 78-80* Royal Doulton revolving cheese dish. Three photographs to illustrate the way it operates. Impressed mark (Godden 1343) IVORY 11.90. Painted in red 675 and also impressed LEACH PATENT c.1890. (Courtesy Mrs M Prest)

*Fig* 59 Shelley Pottery "Tulip" cheese dish 7045 from the pattern book in the Royal Doulton Archives 1898.

*Fig 60* Shelley cheese dish 7022 in two shades of blue 1898. (Courtesy Royal Doulton Ltd)

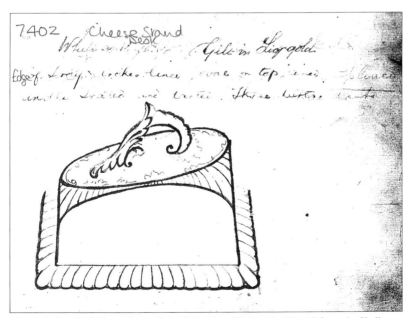

*Fig 61* Shelley desk shape cheese dish 7402 white gilded in liquid gold from the Shelley pattern book 1898-c1922.

## Shelley Pottery Ltd

The following designs and descriptions are reproduced from the Shelley black pattern book C294 dated 24/5/1898 - by courtesy of Royal Doulton Ltd.

**7045** Tulip cheese stand painted in shades of yellow and golden green. (Fig 59)

**7046** as 7045 but painted in French grey shaded in the same colour. Heliotrope tulips with pink centre.

**7022** the same shape with light blue shapes (no flowers) on dark blue background. (Fig 60)

**Desk shaped cheese stands** - two sizes large and small.

Same basic shape for all the following decorations. (Fig 61)

## 1898

**7270** "Festoon of Roses."

**7277** The embossment on the cover and the edge of the base gilded in liquid gold.

**7278** The handle only is gilded with burnished gold.

The following Shelley cheese dishes are from the Doulton Archives No R2.68 dated 15/7/1922.

The same Desk shape as above is still being modelled in two sizes - decorated as follows:

**7402** modelled in white with the arches and the edge of the base lined with liquid gold.

**7495** slate white ground with a lithograph of poppies - gilded.

**7508** slate white ground with a lithograph of roses - gilded.

**Silver Shape Cheese Stand** (Shape No 661)

**7771** Produced in white traced in liquid gold. (Fig 62)

The factory used various printed marks.

## Beswick

Beswick, who were established in 1894, concentrated on producing ornamental ware such as vases and jugs but in the early 1930s added ornamental tablewares to the range. These included some wedge shaped cheese dishes, modelled by Mr Symcock, in

*Fig 62* Shelley "Silver Shape" cheese dish 7771, shape 661 white traced in liquid gold. From Doulton Archives R 2.68 dated 15/7/1922. Introduced February 1912.

*Fig 64* Beswick "Cottage Ware" cheese dishes form a pre-war catalogue 1934-1971. (Courtesy Royal Doulton Ltd)

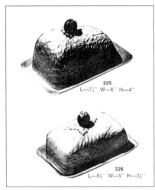

*Fig 63* Beswick "Salad Ware"
cheese dishes from a pre-war
Beswick catalogue c.1930-1972.
(Courtesy Royal Doulton Ltd)

"Salad Ware" - a range of lettuce leaf embossed ware (Fig 63, 225 & 226) and in "Cottage Ware" (Fig 64, 273). Mr White added three larger versions to the "Cottage Ware" range, the largest being in the form of a log cabin (Fig 64, 250, 251 & 252). These dishes were popular and remained in production until 1972.

Other Beswick designs included:

"Country Scene Ware" modelled by Mr Fletcher 1934-40
"Sundial Ware"       modelled by Mr Watkin   1937-54
"Willow Ware"        modelled by Mr Watkin   1937-54
"Petit Point Ware"   modelled by Mr Owen     1938-54
These were not illustrated.

In 1940 "Wayside Ware" was introduced and Mr Watkin modelled two variations of this range - the second in 1941. The range was withdrawn in 1965 (Fig 65, 872, 873).

In 1969 Beswick Ltd was purchased by Royal Doulton Ltd and production from this date concentrated on figures and animals as tableware was phased out.

The ware is printed or impressed B & S or BESWICK.

**Minton Secessionist Wares**

Between 1902 and 1914 Minton produced a range of secessionist wares. The name comes from a group of Viennese artists who founded a secession movement to protest against conservatism in Art. They exerted an influence on decorative arts throughout Europe until the 1920s. Minton secessionist designs were relief-moulded, slip-trailed or block-printed using Majolica glazes. Colours were mustard, pink, purple, red, blue, green and brown which were more subdued than the earlier Majolica colours. Minton produced a wedge shaped cheese dish (shape No 3482)

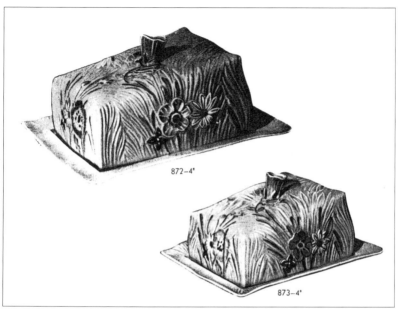

*Fig 65* Beswick "Wayside Ware" cheese dishes from a Beswick catalogue 1940-1965. (Courtesy Royal Doulton Ltd)

*Fig 66* Copeland "Spode's Tower" cheese dish on "Gadroon" shape 1906. (Courtesy Spode Museum Trust)

10.5" by 8.5", with a moulded outline and slip-trailed, in this ware. No illustration, unfortunately, is available but the ware should be marked Minton.

### W T Copeland (& Sons) Ltd

In 1906 Copeland registered two shapes of cheese stand, "Gadroon" and "Cheshire", both also called "Hygienic" and both decorated with under-glaze blue prints.

Fig 66 shows Spode's Tower pattern on the Gadroon cheese stand, while Plate 81 illustrates this pattern on Copeland's "Cheshire" shape. The Tower pattern was originally introduced by Spode in 1814 and shows the bridge of Salaro taken from aquatint engravings which appeared in *"Merigot's Views of Rome and its Vicinity"* published 1796-98.[4]

### Wedgwood

Around the turn of the century Wedgwood produced a very attractive "S" line Stilton cheese stand which is illustrated in Colour Plate 57. This was decorated by a process known as tube-lining which was introduced to the potteries in 1895 by Harry Barnard. In 1896 he moved to Wedgwood and began to decorate some of their ware by tube-lining which they called "S" line. However, after a few years Wedgwood decided to discontinue the process. The technique of tube-lining is rather similar to decorating a cake in that a bag is filled with liquid clay (slip) which is then squeezed through a narrow glass tube to make a thin line on the pottery. This line prevents the colours used in the decoration from running together but also adds to the decorative appearance. Tube-lining is a highly skilled technique.[11] (page 71)

In the early 20th century Wedgwood was still producing Stilton cheese stands in Lavender Ware (introduced 1850s) and also stands decorated with bas-reliefs in three sizes, 6", 5" & 4" diameter. Wedge shaped cheese dishes included Lavender Ware and two blue prints, "Willow" and "Fallow Deer". All would be clearly marked.

*(4) Robert Copeland*
*(11) Bernard Bumpus "Charlotte Rhead. Potter & Designer"*
*Published by Kevin Francis Publishing Ltd London 1987*

*Plate 81* Copeland "Hygienic" "Cheshire" shape cheese stand with "Gadroon" edge. Registered 18th September 1906 (Rd No 487291). Impressed COPELAND and printed mark COPELAND SPODE'S TOWER ENGLAND 1906-c1940. Height 12.5 cm. Width 16.25 cm. Length 22.5 cm.

*Plate 82* Moorcroft Pottery "Blue Porcelain" impressed with the Royal mark 1929-1945.

# Miscellaneous Goods *(Continued.)*

### BEST WHITE BODY.

| | White Glaze | Burnished Gold Lines | Liquid Gold Lines | Coloured and Gold Edge | Gold Clouded |
|---|---|---|---|---|---|
| | s. d. | s. d. | s. d. | s. d. | s. d. |
| Cheese Dish, Carlisle Shape, large size ... each | 4 6 | 6 6 | 5 9 | 6 . 6 | 11 . 0 |
| ,, ,, small size ... ,, | 3 0 | 4 9 | 4 0 | | 7 . 0 |
| ,, *MADELEY* | 2 6 | | | | |
| Cheeses, Douro shape, large size ... ,, | 5 6 | 9 6 | 8 0 | | |
| ,, ,, small size ... ,, | 3 6 | 6 0 | 5 0 | | |
| Cheese Dish, Shell Shape, large size ... ,, | 5 6 | 9 6 | 8 0 | | 11 0 |
| ,, ,, small size ... ,, | 3 0 | 5 6 | 4 6 | | 7 0 |
| Cheese Dish, Corea Shape, large size ... ,, | 5 6 | 7 6 | 6 9 | | |
| ,, ,, small size ... ,, | 3 0 | 5 0 | 4 3 | | |
| | | | | |  Litho and Liquid Gold Edge |
| St. Ivel " Blue Abbey," 2/- each. 1/6 | | | | | |
| St. Ivel Cheese, small size ... ,, | 1 4 | | 2 0 | | 2 6 |

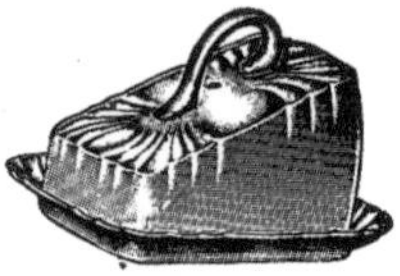

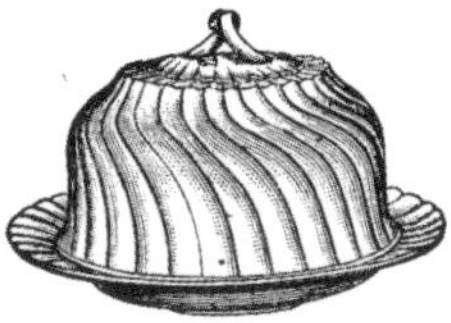

*CRUET TRENTHAM 3 - 3 . 6 P S M*

*Fig 67* George Jones "Crescent Ware" from a catalogue dated February 1923. (Courtesy Wedgwood Museum Trust)

After the 1939-45 war Wedgwood was the only firm to continue production of Stilton cheese stands in Jasper. These are still produced today for special orders.

## George Jones & Sons

In the early 1920s George Jones produced a range of Crescent Ware and in the Wedgwood archives at Barlaston there is a copy of a *Scale Book of Earthenware and China and Price List of Miscellaneous Articles* which is dated February 1923. Figure 67 reproduces a page from this book and shows five shapes of cheese dish which were in production with a hand-written reference to a sixth shape "Madeley" which is not illustrated. The small St Ivel dish had a blue lithograph decoration showing a picture of an abbey.

Also in the Wedgwood archives is *The Crescent Catalogue - George Jones & Sons* which, it is believed, was produced in the 1920s and early 1930s. Figure 69 reproduces (page 88) a "Carlisle" shape cheese dish and cover decorated with "Old English Abbey" pattern *"printed in rich, dark blue from the original engravings"* which was produced in two sizes. Another covered cheese dish is illustrated (page 96) showing the "Athens" shape which was made in three sizes. (Fig 68)

Some of these shapes, especially "Duoro", appear in the Army and Navy Stores catalogues of this period indicating that probably considerable quantities of cheese dishes were produced by this firm.

## William Adams & Sons Ltd

Adams produced Jasperware Stilton cheese stands in the second half of the 19th century but these were still in production in the early 20th century as they were included in their 1904 catalogue. They were made in three sizes: Diameter of base 9.5", 10", 11"; Height of cover (including knop) 5", 6", 7". They were decorated with the Hunting scene illustrated in Figure 70 but could also be decorated with Coats of Arms, Festoons, Dancing Maidens and other classical subjects. They were impressed ADAMS.

*Fig 69* George Jones "Old English Abbey" pattern "Carlisle" shape made in two sizes. Crescent catalogue 1920/30s.

*Fig 68* George Jones "Athens" shape from the Crescent catalogue 1920/30s.

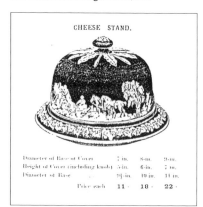

*Fig 70* William Adams jasperware "Hunting" Stilton cheese stand from his 1904 catalogue. (Courtesy Dr D Furniss)

*Fig 71* William Adams "Chinese Bird" cheese dish registered number 623294. From Record of show cards, adverts and publicity notices of the firm in the Wedgwood Archives. (Courtesy Wedgwood Museum Trust)

*Fig 72* William Adams a section of "Titian" design.

Wedge shaped cheese dishes were also produced in three very popular patterns.

*"Chinese Bird"* - this pattern was introduced in 1780 copying a Chinese pattern and was later registered as Patent No 623294. (Fig 71)

*"The Adams original Blue Print"* - rural scenes including animals in underglaze blue print.

*"Titian"* - this was produced in a cream glazed body with a border of green leaves and deep yellow flowers. (Fig 72)

## Moorcroft Pottery - 1930s

I am very grateful to Miss Beatrice Moorcroft for the very clear and interesting account of the production of Moorcroft cheese stands and for her permission for me to reproduce the history here.

Cheese dishes were produced, with other tableware, in the speckled blue slip ware known as "Blue Porcelain", by William Moorcroft before his death in 1945 and by his son, Walter Moorcroft from 1945 to 1963, when production of the tableware was abandoned after fifty years.

A price list printed in the 1930s includes cheese dishes with the other blue tableware. They are priced at 4/- each or 48/- a dozen, but, whereas most of the tableware was in general production, comparatively few cheese dishes were made in the 1930s, and were probably only made to order. Two shapes were available, an oblong dish, and a round dish with a domed lid. Cheese dishes were also occasionally decorated in the characteristic Moorcroft style, on request, e.g. it is known that two decorated dishes were made for Henry Birks of Toronto, Canada, in 1933, to meet a special order. One of them was decorated in a leaf design under a salt glaze and the other in "Autumn Leaf" design, probably under a flambé glaze. Others were produced in very limited numbers and, if any have survived, they would be of exceptional interest to collectors as unique pieces.

The oblong dish shown in Plate 82, now in a private collection, carries the "Royal Mark", the impressed mark adopted after William Moorcroft received the Royal Appointment, as Potter to Her Majesty Queen Mary in 1928. It was therefore made between 1929 and about 1945, the year of his death. The dish was, nevertheless, designed earlier at a date that has not been established. Examples prior to 1929 carried the impressed mark "Moorcroft Made In England", a policy revived by Walter Moorcroft after 1945. The blue tableware was not signed but the rare decorated cheese dishes would have been signed by William Moorcroft, like other decorated Moorcroft pottery of the period.

The "Blue Porcelain" tableware was introduced in 1913, at William Moorcroft's works at Cobridge, as a "bread and butter line" to supplement the decorated pottery that was more expensive to make. It became popular at home and abroad, but in the 1930s it was highly regarded by disciples of the modern movement, many of whom regarded ornament as decadent in this country. For example, in 1934 Herbert Read chose a Moorcroft blue teaset as an example of modern industrial art, *"embodying the tradition of simplicity, precision and appeal of pure form"*[12] and writing in 1937, Sir Niklaus Pevsner, described the blue tableware as, *"essentially modern"*.

Others followed suit and the demand for the tableware accounted to a considerable extent for the survival of Moorcroft Pottery in the world wide trade depression of the early '30s, during which time a limited number of blue cheese dishes were made as components of the blue dinner sets.

### S Fielding & Co

As already noted Fielding produced cheese stands during the 1880s and 1890s and was still producing examples in the early years of the 20th century. Distinguishing initials of S F & Co are often to be found on their pieces and CROWN DEVON from c.1913 onwards.

*(12) "Art and Industry, The Principles of Industrial Design" Herbert Read, published by Faber and Faber, London 1934*

*Fig 74* Burgess & Leigh 1930s catalogue of "Kitchen Ware".

## BURGESS & LEIGH LTD

The white and gold wedge shaped cheese dish shown in Colour Plate 47 was introduced by Burgess & Leigh in c.1897 and they continued to produce this shape with other decorative treatments until c.1930. (Plate 85 page 111)

Fluted Cheese Stand s/s.

*Fig 73* Burgess & Leigh "Fluted" cheese dish 1920s catalogue.

In 1910 and throughout the 1920s Burleigh white ware was produced and this range of table ware included a wedge shaped dish in two sizes in "Queen Fluted." (Fig 73)

The round cheese stand shown in Figure 74 was first produced in the 1870s when blue and white printed ware was so popular but was discontinued sometime during the 1880s. In the 1930s it was decided to produce it again - in other colours as well as blue - as the "Kitchen Ware" range. It was at this time that the labels were added. This range is still in current production and pink print was added to the range in 1991.

The wedge cheese stand top left in Figure 75 is the "Balmoral" shape. The same basic shape was used for "Zenith" but the "Zenith" handle consisted of a curved stem and leaf.

The 1930s production of wedge shaped cheese stands was based on these two shapes which had been designed by Ernest T Bailey. Both were decorated with "Dawn" and "Bluebell" designs but Balmoral, in addition was decorated with "Moiré" - a simulated silk band. "Dawn" was an Art Deco stylised design in bright colours. All pieces are clearly marked.

### The Denby Pottery Company Ltd

The firm was founded in 1809 by Joseph Bourne. In the early days Denby's output consisted of salt glazed bottles and jars but, as it developed, a reputation for vitreous stoneware was established. Its product range included oven ware, decorated art ware and kitchen ware. Indeed it would seem they made everything except cheese stands. The first reference, in the company's catalogue of 1890, is to Stilton cheese stands:

Terracotta      2/6 Plain      4/- Figured
Glazed          3/- Plain      4/6 Figured
No further details are given nor is there any illustration.

No further reference to cheese stands is made until 1932 when a soft cheese dish is included in "Cottage Blue" ware. (Fig 76)

## C T Maling & Sons Ltd - Newcastle upon Tyne
From the 1870s onwards Malings produced decorated services which included a wedge shaped cheese stand. Demand was reduced in the 1920s. (Plate 86) Various printed marks are used many of which included the letters C T M or CETEM WARE.

## R F Dixon & Co (1916-1929)
Dixon's were London retailers and importers who between 1916-29 had this mark applied on wares which were made for them at the Ruby Porcelain Works in Longton, Stoke-on-Trent. (Plate 87)

## Grimwades Ltd
In 1900 the name of the firm was changed from Grimwade Brothers to Grimwades Ltd and they specialised in the production of very inexpensive cheese stands which were very popular with the Edwardians.

Figure 50 reproduces a page from their 1906 catalogue showing examples which sold at 1/6 (7.5p) each. They frequently registered their shapes.

Their dishes measured approximately 9"x 8" x 4" (22.5 x 20 x 10 cm) and had printed marks.

## Some Novelty Designs
Plates 97 - 101 illustrate some of the amusing and novel ideas produced by various potteries.

*Fig* 75 Burgess & Leigh "Balmoral" shape from the 1930s catalogue.

# SOFT CHEESE DISH

CB 200

*Fig* 76 Denby "Cottage Blue" ware soft cheese dish from 1932 catalogue. (Courtesy The Denby Pottery Co Ltd)

Plate 83 S Fielding & Co printed mark S F & Co ENGLAND over a crown ROYAL DEVON c.1910-1915. Height 13.75 cm. Width 16.25 cm. Length 18.75 cm.

Plate 84 S Fielding & Co Rd No 600413. Printed mark CROWN DEVON S F & Co c.1920. Height 16.25 cm. Length 25 cm.

Plate 85 Burgess & Leigh two decorative treatments on the same mould which was first introduced 1868 (see Colour Plate 49) 1900-1920.

Plate 86 C T Maling printed mark CETEM WARE c.1915-1925. Height 10 cm. Width 16.25 cm. Length 20 cm.

*Plate 87* R F Dixon & Co London retailers (Godden mark 1306)- this cheese dish was made for them by the Ruby Porcelain works, Stoke-on-Trent 1916-1929.

*Plate 88* Myott Son & Co printed mark (Godden 2810) with "semi-porcelain" also printed c.1900.

*Plate 89* Keeling & Co underglaze blue printed transfer registered No 595146. Impressed K & Co 1910-c1920. Height 10 cm. Width 15 cm. Length 18.75 cm.

*Plate 90* Alfred Meakin printed mark (Godden 2590) c.1930. Height 10 cm. Length 20 cm.

*Plate 91* Arthur Wood & Son printed mark on both (Godden 4235) c.1934-1944.

*Plate 92* Burgess & Leigh - printed mark BURLEIGH 1930s.

*Plate 93* Keeling & Co - KEELE 383 printed on ware impressed K & Co c. 1900-1936.

*Plate 94* Ridgways - printed mark (Godden 3310) "Agra" c.1900-1930. Diameter 25 cm. Height 12.5 cm.

*Plate 95* Wood & Sons JUAN printed mark 1910. (Courtesy Hornsea Museum)

*Plate 96* Silver plate cheese dish marked on base V D &
S E P 13292.

*Plate 97* Unattributed pair of Swans.

*Plate 98* Unattributed Shell.

*Plate 99* Wiltshaw & Robinson 1890-1957 retitled Carlton Ware from January 1958. 1930s. Height 12.5 cm. Width 22.5 cm. Length 35 cm.

*Plate 100* Unattributed mice dishes.

It would seem appropriate to conclude almost where we began with the Bell Inn at Stilton but this time in the 20th century.

This lovely old inn, now some 350 years old, was very dilapidated when it was, fortunately, purchased and the new owner restored all the ground floor and made it water-tight. A little later it was sold again and the present owners, two generations of the McGivern family, completed the restoration of the upper floors.

This Stilton cheese stand was produced c.1988 by the London Pottery Company to commemorate the restoration of this interesting and historic Inn. (Plate 152)

*Plate 101* Victorian glass cheese dish.

*Plate 102* London Pottery Company - Bell Inn cheese stand 1988.

# GLOSSARY

**BODY** The ceramic term for the ingredients from which pottery is made e.g. earthenware body, stoneware body.

**CANEWARE** An unglazed cane coloured earthenware used by Wedgwood and other manufacturers from c.1780.

**CREAMWARE** A cream coloured earthenware body.

**EARTHENWARE** Pottery fired below 1200°C. It is opaque and is porous unless covered by glaze.

**ENAMELS** Ceramic colours derived from metallic oxides. They are applied on glaze and the ware is then refired at low temperatures.

**GLAZE** A special kind of glass which will adhere to a clay body rendering it impervious and adding shine.

**INTAGLIO** Any figure or design cut into the surface of the pot.

**PARIAN** A white, normally unglazed, body introduced in the 1840s.

**PEARLWARE** A white earthenware body. Small quantities of cobalt oxide were added to the glaze giving it a bluish tint to help the white appearance.

**SLIP** Pottery clays mixed with water to a creamy consistency.

**SLIP-DIPPING** Covering the whole, or parts, of the exterior of the pot with contrasting coloured slip.

**SPRIGS** Small decorative motifs, made in moulds, for attaching to the surface of ware (sprigging).

**STONEWARE** A vitrified body which is fired between 1200°C and 1300°C. It is very hard, strong, opaque and non-porous. It is therefore unnecessary to add a glaze unless for decorative reasons.

**TERRACOTTA** A red or buff earthenware body which is very porous unless glazed.

**ZAFFRE** An impure cobalt oxide used for underglaze blue and white prints. It gives a dark, opaque blue colour.

# BIBLIOGRAPHY

BUTEN David & Jane Perkins Claney "18th C Wedgwood - a guide to Collectors and Connoisseurs" (Buten Museum of Wedgwood Merion P A 1964)

BERGESEN Victoria "Majolica - British, Continental and American Wares 1851-1915" (Barrie and Jenkins Ltd London 1989)

COPELAND Robert "Spode and Copeland Marks" (Studio Vista London 1992)

CUSHION J P "Handbook of Pottery & Porcelain Marks" 4th Edition (Faber & Faber 1980)

DAWES Nicholas M "Majolica" (Crown Publishers Inc, 201 East 50th St, New York, N Y 10022 1989)

DUDSON Audrey M "Dudson - a Family of Potters since 1800" (Dudson Publications, 200 Scotia Road, Tunstall, Stoke-on-Trent ST6 4JD 1985)

GODDEN Geoffrey A "Encyclopaedia of British Pottery & Porcelain Marks" (Barrie and Jenkins London 1965)

HILL Susan "The Shelley Style - A Collector's Guide" (Jazz Publications Ltd, Stratford on Avon 1990)

IRVINE Louise "Royal Doulton Series Ware Vols 1-4" (Richard Dennis London 1980, 1984, 1986 & 1988)

KARMASON Marilyn with Joan B Stacke "Majolica - A Complete History & Illustrated Survey" (Harry N Abrams Inc N Y 1989)

KELLY Alison "Decorative Wedgwood in Architecture & Furniture" (Born-Hawkes Publishing Ltd, New York 1965)

MAY Harvey "The Beswick Collector's Handbook" (Kevin Francis Publishing Ltd 1986)

WAKEFIELD Hugh "Victorian Pottery" (Herbert Jenkins London 1962)

# INDEX

**INDEX TO COLOUR PLATES**